MW01594872

# SUDDENLY
# V

**Prose Poetry and Sudden Fiction**

**Edited by
Jackie Pelham**

Stone River Press
Houston, Texas

# SUDDENLY
# V

## Prose Poetry and Sudden Fiction

Edited by Jackie Pelham
© 2003

Individual story copyright by authors and used with permission
Book design and typesetting by Jackie Pelham
Cover Design by Jesse Johnson
Introduction by Paul Christensen

The following have or will appear in other publications: "Toward the Source" in *Silhouette to Unheard Music,* Plain View Press; "Signing On" in *Visions International,* Black Buzzard Press; "Target Practice" in *The Redneck Review of Literature.*

Library of Congress Control Number: 2003090288

Printed in the United States of America

Published by

Stone River Press
www.stoneriverpress.com

ISBN 0-9627844-9-4

For Peggy Zuleika Lynch

# Table of Contents

# Foreword

Although we had 91 Texas authors, this was the easiest Suddenly so far. The selection of poetry was in the very capable hands of Christopher Woods who has published widely, and the short stories were chosen by Lila Guzman, whose novels have won great praise. I think you will agree the pieces are a tribute to our Texas authors.

Paul Christensen, one of Texas' most prolific authors, wrote the lovely Introduction and that is greatly appreciated. Stone River Press published his prose poetry book *Blue Alleys* in 2002 and it won the Violette Crown Award sponsored by the Writers League of Texas and Barnes & Noble in Austin. The cover, designed by Jesse Johnson who also designed this cover, won an Award of Merit for graphic design excellence sponsored by the Printing Industries of the Gulf Coast, Inc. and the Printing & Imaging Association of MidAmerica. As usual, Mark and the group at Morgan Printing in Austin did the beautiful printing and binding.

The authors in *Suddenly V* are from all across Texas and range in expertise from writers who have been published extensively, to a high school senior who submitted to a publication for the first time. I am so proud of this book that it breaks my heart to say that it will be the last one for awhile. With all my "irons" there isn't time to put it together. I have dedicated this issue to Peggy Zuleika Lynch, dear friend and poet who deserves recognition for her years of service to the writing community.

Thanks to all of you who have submitted to Suddenly. I hope it has contributed in some small way to those of you who will continue to write, and to those who now enjoy the genres of prose poetry and short short fiction. You have made this five year adventure exciting and worthwhile.

—*Jackie Pelham*

# Introduction

One of the earliest examples of prose poetry is the French poet, Charles Baudelaire's little book, *Spleen de Paris,* published in Paris in 1868. It was his most popular book, outselling his more notorious and daring book of lyric poems, *Les Fleurs du Mal* (The Flowers of Evil). Even so, there was nothing quite like *Spleen* in the history of poetry—it took prose as its medium and subverted it by insinuating a subtle, fragmentary world of dreams into its prosaic language. The language of the newspaper and the encyclopedia, that safe, rational medium of the law, the government's own tongue of authority, was now haunted by dreams and discontinuities drifting up out of the unconscious. Never had poetry been so literal and unfamiliar, and never had prose seemed like such a tool of clowns and drugged nightclub vamps preaching impossible dreams. But *Spleen* was a generation ahead of its time, anticipating the coming of the Modernist revolt, and later, of postmodernism's attack on language as a mode of self-delusions.

Each country has since turned the prose poem into something new. In the hands of the Germans, it is a surreal voice of journeys into the unknown self; in England, it became a bitingly satirical assault upon the system of social classes; in America, it has taken the pragmatic self and made a genial drunk out of it. But in the Southwest, it allowed writers who feel repressed by the rigors of lyric poetry to tell their most personal stories. And the stories told in *Suddenly V* represent a female encyclopedia of women's emotions and visions. Of the 91 poets included here, 70 are women. It shouldn't surprise us that women dominate this and many other collections of contemporary writing—as I wrote in my recent memoir, *West of the American Dream: An Encounter with Texas,* women invented lyric voices in the state, laid down the laws of poetry, established reading clubs and libraries, and reconciled themselves with the wild nature of these prairies and river valleys. Men followed, and caught up by the 1980s, but women still rule the written word, as they do here.

As far as I can tell, the majority of writers here are of the boomer generation, and are now passing into middle age. They reflect upon a vanished culture of grandparents on small farms, their own parents' move to the big cities and the suburbs, and now have memories of their own, and empty nests to come home to. There are betrayals, marital anxieties, aging, of course; one or two poems of men and women sexually assessing each other, with surprising frankness and humor. One particularly poignant tale, "Bait," by Pauline Delaney, tells of taking her old mare out to the woods to be used as bear bait for the hunters. Like any good prose poem, it reaches down into our myths and taboos and shakes us hard. Only one poem, Hallie Moore's "Ablution," experiments with language itself, and with good effect.

Hardly anyone follows Baudelaire's example of turning prose inside out, bursting its rational pretensions. The prose here is conventional, a medium for talking out one's frustrations, peeves, desires, or cause for wonder. Even so, something of the soul of the Southwest is bared in these vignettes and sketches of ordinary life. A woman observes a mother and son arguing in Houston traffic in Beth Miles' "Lost in North Houston," as a son runs away down an alley, leaving the mother shouting angrily. She observes her own son beside her "with a tug of gratitude." A boy discovers his father in bed with his homosexual lover after his mother's funeral, in Alvaro Rodriguez' short story "Orion's Belt." And in Sue Volk's story, "Interrupted Dreams," the thud of a half-frozen derelict on a woman's porch turns out to be her own son.

The violence of contemporary America seems just below the surface. The alienation of the city and the suburbs, the slowly crumbling condition of the family, the subtle and acidic disintegration of marriage in our time are all recounted here in stories and poems. It is, by and large, an unhappy world viewed through these many eyes. Things are not right, the center keeps falling further from our lives, as we go sprawling in an age of social incoherence. But here and there you find garden meditations, celebrations of things as simple as a few sunflowers blooming against a fence, a black woman's understanding heart, in Thomas Spiriti's short story "Sarah's Detour." Or the masterful evocation of an old pump jack in James Hoggard's poem, "The River on Us."

This edition of Jackie Pelham's series of Suddenly anthologies is intriguing, and leads us into that invisible Texas writers flesh with their words. It is a place of longing and loneliness eased occasionally by a pet cat or an old dog, a stranger with penetrating eyes, a garden growing on the edge of a city hall, or some other reminder that we live on forgiving land that feeds and comforts us. The effect of so much honesty and self-reflection is reassurance that Americans are not just consumers or blank faces in traffic jams, but feeling and searching people, human beings with strong imaginations and strong dreams, wanting something more, something to feed their hearts and souls with. This body of work has moved me often, and some of the voices I shall remember for a long, long time.

—**Paul Christensen**

**PAUL CHRISTENSEN'S** most recent books are a memoir of Texas life and literature, *West of the American Dream: An Encounter with Texas* (Texas A&M Univ. Press, 2001) and *Blue Alleys,* a collection of prose poems published by Stone River Press, winner of the 2002 Violet Crown Award for Literature from the Writers' League of Texas. He teaches writing and modern literature at Texas A&M University.

# Poetry Judge

**CHRISTOPHER WOODS** writes fiction, non-fiction, poetry and plays. He is the author of *The Dream Patch*, a lyrical novel about a Texas family during the 1940's. His collection of prose poems and brief fictions, *Under A Riverbed Sky*, was published by Panther Creek Press. His collection of stage monologues for actors and actresses, *Heart Speak*, was published by Stone River Press.

His play *Murmurs* was produced recently at the Sol Theatre Project in Fort Lauderdale. *Murmurs* is based on his book *Heart Speak*. He also recently received a Pushcart Prize nomination for a story that appeared in *Whalelane*.

His work has appeared in over four hundred publications in the U.S. and in fourteen foreign countries. These publications include *Columbia, The Southern Review, New England Review, Confrontation, Rosebud* and *Glimmer Train*.

His plays have been produced in Houston, Fort Worth, Memphis, Minneapolis, Providence, Boston, Chicago, Los Angeles, New York, Tampa and Santa Fe. They include *A Woman on Fire,* about a woman who survives a fire in which her husband and child perish; *Moonbirds,* about doomed census-takers at work in a Third World country; *Interim,* about souls in Purgatory. *Pillow Dreams,* a drama about Alzheimer's and matricide, *La Loma,* about a young American in a Mexican prison; *This Way to the Beds, Ladies and Gentlemen,* monologues and duets on the theme of sheets, real and metaphorical. His monologue shows include *Women Alone* for actresses, and *Lover, Killer, Angel, Thief* for actors.

He has received a grant from the Mary Roberts Rinehart Foundation, and has received residencies at the Ucross Foundation in Wyoming and the Edward Albee Foundation in New York. He lives in Houston where he has taught creative writing workshops at Rice University Continuing Studies Program, The Women's Institute, and by correspondence.

# Fiction Judge

**LILA GUZMAN** writes short stories and novels from her home in Round Rock, Texas. She holds a Ph.D. in Spanish literature and a commission in the United States Navy. At the Defense Language Institute in Monterey, California, she trained speakers to teach their language to military personnel in all branches of the service. She received a Joint Service Commendation Medal in May 1983.

Her first short story "Star Apples" won honorable mention in fiction from the National League of American Pen Women to which she has recently become a member of the Bluegrass Chapter.

Lila has won numerous writing awards since. Her short stories have appeared in *San Diego Writers Monthly, Millennium Science Fiction and Fantasy, Xoddity,* the *Roswell Literary Review, Canadian Writer's Journal, Arizona Literary Magazine* and other publications.

In September 1999 she began a free e-newsletter for novice writers called "Ask the Author." It now goes out to subscribers worldwide and has a circulation of 3200.

In Lila's first children's novel *Green Slime and Jam* (Eakin Press, 2001), three literary characters are whisked from their books by a mysterious green slime.This award-winning fantasy novel introduces children to forgotten classics.

*Lorenzo's Secret Mission* (Arte Publico Press, 2001), is a collaboration between Lila and her husband Rick. An action-packed young adult novel, it tells the story of the Spanish contribution to the American Revolution in 1776.

The sequel *Lorenzo's Revolutionary Quest* (Arte Publico, 2003), deals with Texas's role in the American Revolution.

Lila is a frequent speaker at schools and conferences. In addition, she runs a fiction-critiquing service. Visit her website at *www.talkto/Lila* for more information.

# Poems and Stories

# V. T. ABERCROMBIE

## *Signing On*

*You write your name the same each time now. We can open you a checking account,* my father said. My signatures, sprawled across the bottom of each check—clothes, midnight pizzas to doctor bills, groceries, mortgage payments all spawn the same checkbook look. In mother's desk I found a book, small, dated 1911-1917, called "My Friends," filled with signatures written perpendicular on the page, each folded while the ink was wet. Like a Rorsach test, dragons, butterflies, angels engaged the inky names. I imagine each looped L, each turn of a P, duplicating itself through World War I, The Great Depression; the way soldiers are taught to march holding arms at a just-so angle. Given substance one could stack a life's worth of signatures one over the other, could see all the way down through the O's and D's to the beginning of it all. Whether cursive or print, we lock ourselves to life by the slant of an A, the swirl of a B, the curve of an S, by the butterflies and dragons and angels on yellowed paper and the trail of signature bones behind us.

## *Apparition of a Lost Love*

She sensed his presence, especially at night, when she'd feel the impression of his body next to her and the wind of his icy breath blowing softly across her cheeks. On occasion, she'd even see him. A chill would seize her and she'd look up and there he'd be, standing in the doorway or outside the clear glass of the shower stall, watching her. After a few seconds, he'd disappear, leaving a momentary after-image of light. She never tried to talk to him because she was afraid he might answer.

JUNE ADLER

# Mary's House

Rob met Mary at a singles bar. She was a stunning girl—
long auburn hair, ultramarine blue eyes, and a body a guy
would steal his mother's purse for. Yet there was something
about Mary that made him uneasy, something Rob couldn't
quite put his finger on. But, because of her other considerable
attributes, he shoved those feelings aside when Mary invited
him for dinner.

Rob arrived at her door promptly at eight the following
evening, a red rose in hand.

Mary answered the door dressed in a long white robe.
Behind her in the entry hall, dozens of candles flickered in
the dim light.

She led him into the stucco-walled living room. The
only furnishings were a carved rosewood altar and six black
floor pillows. More lit candles rimmed the perimeter of the
room. She took the red rose out of his hand and placed it on
the altar, bowing her head briefly.

"Is this a church or something?" Rob asked.

"In a sense, YES, and in a sense NO," Mary said.
"Come."

Rob followed her into the kitchen where candles
flamed between the burners on the stove and on the dust-
laden top of the refrigerator. A smaller altar sat on the kitchen
table guarded by a pair of lion-shaped salt and pepper shakers.

"You really like candles," Rob said.

"They give me a sense of serenity. Follow me. I want
you to see my bedroom."

Desire flicked across Rob's face as Mary led him into
a black-walled room. He could see from the light cast by the

21

lavender-scented candle floating in a glass bowl on a night stand, that the only other piece of furniture was a low bed covered with a leopard print throw.

"Don't you watch TV or anything?"

"No. This house is my sanctuary, my retreat from the outside world—a place to perform my rituals."

"What kind of rituals?" Rob asked, a sudden chill seizing him.

"You know—my food rituals, my prayer rituals—my bathing ritual.

"Oh—those rituals."

"I haven't shown you my bathroom yet."

Rob followed Mary down a dark hallway to a half-opened door. He stepped inside. The walls of her bathroom were painted a blood red, but what really caught his attention was the double sized Jacuzzi, filled with bubbling, steaming water. Next to the tub, on an ornate pedestal, a brass-plated candelabrum sent flickers of light across the room. Rob's spirits lifted, until he noticed with a stab of horror, that lying in the pristine white sink to the left of the tub was a man's head sealed in a clear plastic bag.

"Oh my God!" he cried, and clutched at his chest.

"Don't be frightened! It's just a fiberglass prop for a movie I'm working on. See?" She undid the zip-lock bag, exposing part of the forehead and a tuft of black curly hair.

"What's it doing in your sink?" Rob asked, taking a step back. His breathing came in rough gasps.

"It was just a silly joke. I thought it would make you laugh."

"It looks so real," he said, holding his hand over his accelerated heart and licking his dry lips.

"Well, its not. Listen, I thought you might want a bath before dinner. Why don't you take your clothes off and get into the tub while I check on the food. I'll be right back to give you a nice back-rub."

Mary walked out of the bathroom, bagged head in hand, and closed the door behind her.

Rob's heart jumped when he heard a second click. For a moment he thought she had locked him in. He tried the door and felt foolish when it opened.

Regaining his composure, he hurriedly stripped off his clothes and stepped into the still steaming tub. He sank down into the soothing waters until its heat caressed his earlobes. He closed his eyes and imagined Mary in the tub with him. He opened them again when sounds of organ music swelled up out of the silence.

Standing in the doorway, the reflections of the flickering candles dancing across her pale skin, was Mary, a ravishing naked goddess—clutching a large rusty ax in her right hand.

Rob rose up out of the water, screaming.

She started to laugh hysterically, her eyes shining red in the candlelight. "You're such a fraidy cat," she spit out between her laughter. "It's just rubber. See?" She thrust the ax at him.

Shaking and sobbing, Rob cowered in the tub—shrieking, each time Mary moved toward him.

"Men nowadays don't have any sense of humor," she said. Then, with an impish smile, she stared into Rob's terror stricken orbs and blew out the candelabrum flames one by one.

## ANN ANDERSON

## *Six Young Lions*
## *First Day At Masai Mara*

Apricot glow paints the sky and flows onto the Masai Mara plain of Kenya. Animals mingle in undulating beauty. Was the world so when the lion lay down with the lamb?

In luminous twilight, zebra and wildebeest graze red oat grass, grunting. Tiny gazelles head butt and spring into the air, appreciative of life. Birds welcome a sliver of sun. Four giraffe rock across a hillside, silhouettes.

A slice of sunlight glides forward, touches an acacia tree, turning it from shadow to dusky green; highlights a topi, bringing its red-brown body into sharp relief, revealing black face markings that give it the name devil's beast. The beam widens, hurries, tinting the mist gold, the sky bright orange, then slides into dark ravines to spotlight herds of Grant's gazelle and impala, wart hogs and buffalo.

Black vervet monkeys, wakened by the sudden blaze, screech to life in a fig tree and a mongoose family shoot up, one at a time, blinking in the glare. The sun rises more swiftly now, hauling its great bulk away from the weight of the hillside into the airy freedom of the sky.

The cooling veil dissolves to reveal a parched land. And there, purring on a hillock, lie six young lions.

# ANN ANDERSON

## *Rag Doll*

**I** was sittin in the old red rocking chair with Granpa, eating slices of apple he cut with his pocket knife, when the doc came banging at the screen door, callin for Granma.

"Need your help delivering Sally Sue's baby, Emma Mae. She's not but a child herself and that mother of hers is drunk as usual. I need someone dependable."

Granma put the sock she was knitting on the wooden dining table, pushed out of her rocking chair and smoothed her cotton print apron as she walked to the door. "What happened to that new County nurse?" she asked him, face to face through the screen.

"Got impetigo on her hands from treating the Witt boys. Can't let her touch a newborn."

Granma nodded and turned to Granpa. "You look after Mary Ann?"

Granpa waved the hand holding the pocketknife, then cut me another slice of apple and one for himself. I was sitting sideways, with my legs under the gold-trimmed arm of the rocking chair and my skinny back up against Granpa's side. I had Annie, my rag doll, sleepin on my lap. I smiled up at Granpa and decided to ask if we could go play with the new baby rabbits he kept in hutches in the chicken yard when we finished the apple.

Well, we played with the rabbits, all right, and fed the chickens and Granma still wasn't back. She didn't get back 'til it was coal black outside and way past suppertime. I'd already fed my doll and put her to bed.

Seems the young'un took a mind to come out backwards and Doc Eberhardt had a hard time getting it turned around. Grandma said it was nigh-on-to being blue when it did get born but the old doc had his tricks, and next thing you know, it started screaming like all get out.

"Gonna call her Julie," Granma said.

The rest of the summer seemed to fly by what with new Rhode Island Red peepies coming and growing into fryers and rabbits getting butchered and carried off to market. Next thing you know, we had butternuts and walnuts to hull and a whole garden of vegetables to pick and can.

The first snow was falling and it was pretty near dark when Sally Sue came a screamin and poundin on the back door. "Help me. Oh Jeasus god help me, Emma Mae. It's my Julie. She ain't breathing. Come on.... Come on." She dragged at Granma's arm. She wasn't but sixteen or seventeen, and her long red hair was tangled and wild looking, just like her eyes.

Granma grabbed a babushka and wrapped it around her shoulders. I started to follow, but Gran grabbed my arm hard and told me to stay put. I could tell she wouldn't brook no nonsense, so I did as I was told.

Wasn't more than fifteen minutes Gran was back, white as a sheet. Granpa took her into the living room to sit down 'fore she fainted. I could tell from the set of her mouth it wasn't good news, so I stood real quiet by the doorway and held Annie tight to my chest.

"Seems little Julie was crying all night and most of today. Teething, I expect. Sally Sue says her mother'd only had a beer or two when she insisted on taking the baby into the bedroom at the other end of the house so Sally Sue could get some sleep. When Sally Sue wakened up, Eleanor was gone and little Julie was quiet."

Granma started cryin then. I could hardly understand her, but once I figured out what she was sayin, I never forgot.

"Oh that poor baby. Her neck's broke, Harold. My guess is Edna shook her to stop her crying. Probably didn't

26

mean to hurt her. But when I picked her up, her head rolled around like a rag doll's. That's just what she felt like. A rag doll."

Frightened, I dropped Annie and, scared I'd hurt her, picked her up again right quick. Her head lolled back and I pictured little Julie. It took Gran a whole hour to stop my crying and carryin on. By then, nobody wanted supper any more.

# *Morning, September 11*

**I** believed in night—the moon's river of poured silk, like fingers of God, seeping the crevices of desire, a night drenched with magic enough to open the Moonvine and the mind latticed with living. I believed night was a time chosen to preamble a new story, that book of morning that glows without candle flicker, its pages turning forward on hinges of hope and the spatial emptiness bequeathed by a Texas dawn—until I saw into the blackness of lost wills driving headlong into a destruction of more than themselves by a learned devotion to death.

I believed in dawn, pale crops of peace unfolding from the natural fear of dreams before the eyes are ready. I embraced it as a lover who holds even the homely close, until I witnessed the scales that balance the routine of living tipped by an obsessive infatuation with the coffin of a morning assigned to its hour.

And I believed in sleep as planned in its approach as constellations on their ordained path, sleep as healing as the balm poured from Mary's alabaster jar, until the startling edge of abomination severed fulfillment from the promise of happiness, closing down the dreams behind untold eyelids warped open forever.

## NICK ARGUELLO

# *I Opened My Eyes*

**I** opened my eyes. I saw the faint glow of the alarm clock, but not the numbers themselves, having turned it that way intentionally. Waking in the middle of the night had become a pretty regular occurrence. If past experience was any guide, it was about four o'clock.

I rolled over on my other side and stretched in a different direction for a few short minutes, once to the right, once to the left, then repeated the process. A way to give my body's short-term memory a different feel, a point of contrast before settling for good on my back.

The moment I turned, her head fell across my arm. It had happened unconsciously, her eyes still closed, the rhythm of her breath unchanged. She used to stir the moment I moved, even if I only twitched. But tonight she lay undisturbed, her breathing so light that even though only an inch separated our faces, I had to strain to catch its rising and falling.

Somewhere, a distant ache began. My body gently requesting that I readjust, that I shift my weight elsewhere. It knew my nightly routine and had grown accustomed to bearing this burden only briefly.

I didn't respond, but it repeated the request, this time using its voice less faintly. As I continued to ignore it, the voice took on more and more urgency. Move, it told me, sending signals here and there, one aimed at my neck, another at my hip, a knee, a forearm, even my head being used to express its discontent.

Most nights I obeyed promptly. But tonight I remained still. Tonight the pain wouldn't matter. How long had it been since I felt that way? How long since I had made that same choice for anyone, for any of those that had lain in that same spot before her? How long since I decided that allowing one of them to rest undisturbed was more important than this momentary discomfort, this lost sleep?

And what did it mean? Had she become that important to me? If so, when did that happen? Just tonight? And did I mean it? Or was it just that there was too much untapped affection within me, too much desire to make someone beside myself a priority and that she was just an outlet for that?

It seemed such a small gesture, but an important one for me. I hadn't changed cities for someone else's career. I hadn't stayed unflinchingly by someone's side through a terminal disease. But tonight I had the opportunity to bear this pain and put another's good ahead of my own. And I was meeting that challenge.

I lightly rested my lips against her face. A slight shiver made its way through her fur and a low purr rumbled from her belly. I returned to my back, closed my eyes and wondered who I would make that decision for the next time.

# Toy Soldiers

**I** stare at my stuff piled in the empty apartment. Faye needs her space, she says. "Irreconcilable differences," her lawyer calls it. I thought she HAD space, with an income of six figures, unlimited travel, all the expensively tailored suits she can ever wear and her own key to the executive washroom.

It's not about what she needs; it's about what she doesn't need.

Me.

Ben calls. "Frank? Faye's flying to New York this morning. My God, that may be her flight!"

I rush over and find her father, looking at the TV, shaking uncontrollably. We call the airlines and hug like a couple of scared kids until she calls. He holds the phone so I can hear.

"Hi, Pop. I'm okay. I can see the smoke from my hotel room. We're trying to locate family members. Another hour and I would have been on that floor."

"Frank's here. Do you want to talk to him?"

I reach for the phone.

"No, I'll call when I can get a flight. Bye."

He notices my stunned look. "She's worried about all her friends, that's all."

"It's okay, Ben. She's got a lot on her plate and she doesn't need my baggage."

"You'll never be baggage, Frank."

"Tell her that."

I trudge home and watch CNN, the posturing politicians, the talking-head experts, the steely eyes of the crazed killers. I wonder what kind of monster can slaughter innocent people like that in the name of God.

It certainly doesn't please MY God!

I have nightmares of mass murderers with the blood of six thousand human beings dripping from their fangs, as they go to their reward in Paradise. Their cloven hooves desecrate the golden street. They dance and sing, Belafonte-like, "Hey, Mr.Taliban, tally up me virgins!"

I awake soaking wet. Was I screaming?

As I arrange things on my desk, I notice a familiar pewter figurine.

I pick Patriot Joe up and examine him. His flintlock rifle is broken off at his fist. His paint has long since worn away, exposing shiny metal. Occupying a spot on my desk since my college years, his three-cornered hat at a jaunty angle, he brandishes his shattered rifle. The sight of him always inspires me to write heroic words.

I call Ben to ask about Faye. No news.

On TV I see lone figures plunging through the smoke toward certain death. I watch the slow-motion collapse and the huge antenna plunges into its own rubble like an arrow to the heart.

I see exhausted, brave men crawling into dark and dangerous places, looking for pieces of the dead.

I scan the scurrying people for a glimpse of Faye. She probably has a command post set up, giving orders like a platoon sergeant.

I come upon an old crushed box. The duct tape is curled and coming loose. "OLD PHOTOS, FRANK'S TOY SOLDIERS. " I open it.

Dozens of toy soldiers jumbled together remind me of that day, long ago, when I was leaving for college. On impulse, I had selected Patriot Joe and placed him in my pocket.

As a kid, after many a playtime battle, I packed the soldiers in little camps with their own kind, to lick their wounds. I had packed Indian Joes separate from Cowboy Joes,

32

kept G.I. Joes separate from Japanese and German Joes and Patriot Joes apart from the British and French Joes.

Many moves over the years have jumbled them all together and, like Patriot Joe, their painted uniforms are worn down to the pewter. They are indistinguishable from each other. They are just "Joes".

That black September morning, dubbed appropriately 9-11, metamorphosed whole nations. Suddenly it caused them to lose their distinguishing colors, and put aside their "irreconcilable differences," revealing the same metal underneath in order to take on a brutal, mutual foe.

Inspired, I fire up my long-dormant computer. I write, delete, write again, unaware of the time.

"Hi."

Startled, I look up and see her leaning against the door. She looks tired, clad in jeans and a sweatshirt, no business suit. Sneakers, no stylish heels. No makeup. Her hair is down in desarray. She never looked more beautiful.

I feel uneasy. "Faye. I didn't hear you come in."

"You should be more careful about locking your door."

I ask, "What brings you here?

"You forgot something when you moved out." She produces a bottle of red wine from behind her back. This is the last bottle in the case and it's also my last chance."

"Last chance for what?"

"Frank, I saw that plane hit! I saw it all. The fire, the collapse, everything! I saw the death. I smelled it. It changed me. I don't want to be alone, ever again. Please Frank."

We hold each other. Two frightened people, trying to be sane in an insane world.

She says, "Are you hungry? I brought Chinese."

"Starved!" I say.

Irreconcilable differences? They don't seem so daunting anymore.

I look back at my desk. Patriot Joe remains on guard. I hope he always will.

33

# CAROL BARRETT

## The Boat

We'd hear stories by the fire at Y-Camp that were supposed to make you shiver. Never worked for me, I knew they were made up. It was the true ones that got me, like the winter the Boy Scouts took the boat across Spirit Lake, hit a submerged log and broke bottom. They weren't even wearing life jackets my father complained, as if that could have saved them, as if there was always a way to be saved. Two boys started swimming for shore. The scoutmaster called out into the icy air: Stay with the boat! Stay with the boat! One turned back, the other kept going, dragged himself onto the snowy bank, ran four miles in wet clothes to get help.

When they got there, the boat was underwater, and everything attached to it. It's always the body's decision: when to do what you're told, when to trust your own heartbeat, quivering toward shore.

## D. CREASON BARTLETT

# Clean-up, Aisle Three

Some old lady fell in the store today. She did this sort of finger-in-a-light-socket jitter, like parts of her wanted to turn down the can aisle and other parts wanted to press on toward the meat market. And for a second she wavered as if gravity itself weren't sure which way to go. A swipe and a miss at her shopping cart, then her legs folded under, and she spilled into a pile of housegown and blue-gray hair.

A floor tile popped out of place. I'd been expecting that. I don't know which is in worse shape, this pitiful old mom-and-pop or its old customers who shuffle along in their house slippers, wheezing behind wobbly-wheeled shopping carts.

I tried to remember if I'd mopped up all the water puddles from where the roof leaks and drips—or in some places pours. This hanger-on of a store fills up like a reservoir every time it rains.

Meanwhile, the old lady's driverless shopping cart swerved and crashed drunk into a Pearl beer display. Several six-packs swan-dove to the floor, and a can split open and spewed beer where I was now pretty sure I'd already mopped. At least I was hoping so. The last thing I needed was to be out of a job—pitiful minimum-wage slop-job though it was—with a lawsuit for negligence.

Misty, the cashier on duty, peeked around the cigarette display beside her register. She scanned the old lady, the runaway shopping cart, and the lake of Pearl like they were just another line of items she had to punch up prices for. Then her head disappeared behind the cigarettes, and with the same monotone as when calling for a price check, Misty's voice called over the PA system, "Clean-up, aisle three."

35

By then the old lady was picking herself up, working her joints, testing her legs, clutching the cart. When she saw me standing aside she forced a semi-smile between shivering lips. I saw the flush in the folds of her face and the shame in her shuddering stance. She was embarrassed that I saw her fall. And as I turned toward the stock room to get a mop, the thought registered with me that it should have been the other way around.

We stand by and watch, all just pitiful hangers-on ourselves, waiting for gravity to make up its mind, for someone to come along and mop up after us. I glanced back at the broken tile, the spilled beer, and the old woman wobbling away behind her cart. She did not look back at the mess she'd made, and I did not look forward to cleaning it.

# SUNDAY BENNETT

## *Point Of View*

A plastic bag skipping, sliding and alternately gliding and grating its way across the parking lot. Just an ordinary bag, a mundane thing shoved by an invisible hand. A thing discarded, yet in another world, to those creatures we seldom notice, what is it? Could it be an avalanche of plastic barreling along toward their home? A polymer nightmare, the suffocating refuse of the gods? Or is it a saving piece of mankind, the thing which slips ever so slightly across the curb and provides escape from the elements. Beneath the plastic, warm and dry, a life lives on sheltered from nature in an artificial cocoon of white. Not much to say of a plastic bag, neither good nor ill but how you view it.

OVON ROSS BOOTH

## Life of a Rose—A Microcosm

Picking up scissors and gloves, the woman walked out into the emerging dawn and bent over the rose bushes. The tightly curled scarlet bud was touched by a single drop of dew glistening like a tear on the cheek of a girl just about to enter womanhood. The gardener reached for her scissors to clip the stem of the rose, but drew back and looked ruefully at the speck of blood on her glove where a thorn had pierced it. "Fair enough. You have a right to protect yourself from those who would harm you as a young girl protects herself from predators." The rose was curled tightly, not quite ready to lay bare its heart. Soon the warmth of the sun would woo it into unfurling as a young lady responds to the enticing words of her lover. It will be more radiant in its fully developed state as is a woman in the height of her productive years. Even as its beauty begins to fade, it will have a lingering charm unique to its stage of life, as has a venerated matron, still valued for past contributions. The gardener reached for her scissors once more, then paused, realizing that by cloistering it in a tiny vase, she alone could enjoy its beauty, and its life span would be shortened, but left near the path, every passerby would benefit from its loveliness and fragrance just as a girl who is allowed to reach her full potential makes the world a better place in which to live.

# KAY MERKEL BORUFF

## *Viêt-Nàm Redux*

THE FLAMES RETURNED. Not the flames from Têt, rockets the VC lobbed into Sài-Gòn; not the flames from the monks, immolating themselves to protest the U.S.; not the flames chasing a little naked child; not the flames outside my house, a gasoline truck burning on the freeway. Those flames were close to me; they were my flames. But this time, the flames were far away, in New York, like some movie, violence without sound, replaying in color every hour, like scenes from Southeast Asia shocking U.S. audiences during nightly news. All day, the flames were far away as I graded papers, observing older students reacting to a new world, a world in flames. The flames were far away—until the end of the day, students dismissed, going home to their safe lives. And the flames returned: the fear returned: fear in Taipei, a minority for the first time, surrounded by almond eyes, my round eyes steeling panic behind a perfect wife facade; fear in Udorn, electricity suffering a brown-out; fear living alone in Bangkok; fear burning a body at a Buddhist funeral, smelling the un-embalmed corpse as I threw lighted sticks on the pyre; fear seeing men in camouflage, tanks on the streets in Sài-Gòn; fear when my world shattered with the words—Your husband has been shot down.

# ANN REISFELD BOUTTE

## *Sweethearts*

It was a ritual they never neglected. Each morning before he left for work, she would pluck a tiny, pink sweetheart rose from the trellis in their garden and pin it to his lapel. Some men might have scoffed at the notion of wearing a flower, but he was a free spirit who did what pleased him.

A doctor by profession and fisherman by avocation, he was known for sporting the delicate bloom and would not have seemed dressed without one. Over the years, grateful patients gifted him with lapel pins, often with miniature vases.

No one knew how the ritual had begun. They had met at the wedding of his sister to her brother. Perhaps he was wearing a boutonniere when their eyes met and they knew it was destiny. Or it may have stemmed from whispered endearments or a special place they discovered together. It was a secret they never shared.

But twenty years into her widowhood, her eyes filled with tears when she spoke of her sweetheart. And each time she visited his grave, she'd take a rose plucked from her garden and place it on the ground where she imagined his lapel would be.

## ANN REISFELD BOUTTÉ

# *Maria's Doll*

She hesitated for a moment, then pushed open the door to Gepetto's Doll and Toy Shop. Trembling, she placed a box on the counter and gently opened the lid as the owner looked on. With gnarled fingers, she carefully peeled away layers of tissue.

As though turning back pages in a book, her thoughts returned to Christmas morning, 1957, when her daughter Maria had ripped open the wrapping paper to discover that her wish had been granted. On a satin pillow lay Cissette, a ten-inch Madame Alexander Doll with peaches and cream complexion, black curls and blue eyes framed by thick lashes. She smiled at the memory of joy on her eight-year-old's face as she caressed the dainty figure.

Maria glowed as she inspected the accompanying wardrobe—a black crocheted dress, a navy and pink suit with matching hat, handbag and shoes, a lingerie ensemble, and a silver beaded evening gown and mink stole. Maria's flushed cheeks were the only hint that day of the illness that would take her life the following year, driving the grieving mother to pack the doll in its box, seal it, and set it in the attic where it would remain, undisturbed, for forty-three years.

Deep into her seventies and in declining health, she began to reconsider Cissette. She had no one to leave her to, and she feared that whoever disposed of her possessions would fail to recognize the treasure. Better, she decided, to retrieve the doll, still in pristine condition, and offer it to a shop for consignment. Eyes damp, she took one last look at Cissette, then turned to go.

Days later, a doll collector who wandered into the shop could hardly believe her good fortune.

# The Concert

**B**ill Watson sat down in the cane-bottomed chair and said, "U. R., the last time I was here you said you knew a good Indian story."

I thought a bit and decided I would tell him even if he wouldn't believe it.

"Years ago my grandpa told about Joe Bell, one of our kin who went to Galveston after Texas won independence. He thought he could get a job on one of the barges carrying goods to market and supplies along the Brazos. He asked some people at an auction if they knew where he could apply for a job. A fellow said his best bet was in a grog shop and since he was going there Bell might come along with him. This fellow ordered a 'suasion' drink. It was the worst thing Bell had ever tasted. The bartender laughed and the fellow said, "You ain't seen nothin' yet. Texas has the best of everythin'.

"Who are you?" Joe wanted to know.

"Me? Why I'm the only white man that ever seen singing snakes. I'm Tom Jason, the red-headed son-of-a-gun from up the Brazos way."

A customer asked if Tom could bring more hides on his next trip.

"Can't say." He narrowed his eyes. "All depends on them Indians. They're getting' restless up thar. I don't make friends easy, but I shore made friends with a Tonk."

"When was that?"

"Oh, sometime back." He poured himself another drink. "Yeah, the Tonk's the one that told me about singing snakes."

"I've seen snakes in my time, too." Bell remarked.

42

"Not this kind. I've seen them and I was soberer than a parson." Tom Jason leaned back in the oak chair and began.

"It was like this. I give a Tonk boy some corn pone when I was out huntin'. He was starving. Said his tribe was about gone. We got friendly like and got along fine. We hunted in the place and met often. One day he says, 'Follow me.' And follow him I did. We come to the Gulf shore and he bade me git in a canoe. Wal, you never can trust one of them so I was skittish thinkin' I might git my throat cut. Then he says to me, he says, 'I take you to see the strangest thing in the world, the singing snakes.' I'd heard about them snakes and was kinda anxious to see them so I got in the canoe. We rowed to a little island, hid the canoe and climbed up a slope. The island was rocky. Just a few straggling trees. Then, he told me to stop. He walked about ten paces and took out a sort of reed. He played the sweetest kind of a tune. All of a sudden I heard rattling all around. I beat it for the nearest tree and climbed up. Wal, you never seen such a sight. The snakes gathered before the Tonk and one big rattler took his place in front of the snakes. The little rattlers gathered in one place, medium-sized ones in another, and big ones in another. The big snake signaled with his tail and such a beatin' time to the music you never heard. The big ones was the bass, the mediums played tenor and little 'uns beat out high notes. At the last note, the big snake beat his tail on the ground and they all left. I never seen such a sight"

Bell twirled his glass and said, "Even Texas stories are the greatest."

Tom declared, "It ain't a story. It's the truth."

"Sure, Texans tell only the truth."

I looked over at Bill and he sat there without saying anything for a few minutes, got up, and said, "I'd best be going. I promised the Widow Jones I'd mow her yard."

After he left I latched the screen and remembered—Bill doesn't have a mower.

# MICHAEL BRACKEN

## *All My Yesterdays*

When I was six, I spilled a box of instant rice. My father made me pick it up, grain by grain.

The next morning, my father walked barefoot across the kitchen floor. He called me into the kitchen, showed me the grain of rice stuck to the bottom of his big toe, then backhanded me.

When I cried, he hit me again.

When I was eight, my father drove my mother to the hospital. While x-raying my mother's broken arm, a nurse asked what had happened. My mother looked at my father, then said that she'd fallen down our basement steps.

Our house doesn't have a basement.

When I was ten my father drove over my bicycle.

I'd left it in the driveway in my hurry to use the bathroom. When I finally returned, I saw him carefully and deliberately drive over my year-old Stingray.

He made me clean up the twisted metal pieces before dinner.

When I was twelve, I awoke in the middle of the night to the sound of my father shouting and my mother crying as he hit her.

I stuffed my head under my pillows and tried to sleep.

When I was fourteen, I called my father a name. He slugged me, knocking me into the living room wall. Then he grabbed my shirt collar and dragged me to his bedroom. He pushed me down on the bed. With one hand he opened the drawer of his nightstand, removing a revolver I had seen only once before. He shoved the barrel into my mouth. Between clenched teeth, he whispered, "Don't you ever call me that again."

44

Then he pulled the trigger. The hammer snapped down on an empty chamber, but I had already wet my pants.

Last night, I heard my mother screaming again. I tried to stuff pillows around my head like I had done before, but this time I couldn't muffle the sounds. Then I heard a loud thump against the wall and my mother stopped screaming.

This morning, I woke to find my father cooking breakfast. I asked him where mother had gone.

"Out," he said. "Get ready for school."

My father left before I did, earlier than he'd ever left before. I saw him put a shovel in the car.

While gathering my schoolbooks, I glanced into my parents' bedroom. The bedspread had disappeared and the bed remained unmade. My mother never left the bed unmade. My father wouldn't allow it. I stayed home from school and thought about it.

Early this afternoon, I searched through my father's nightstand and found his revolver. I loaded it.

At five o'clock, I moved the lounge chair into the foyer, facing the front door. I sat in the chair and cradled the heavy gun in my lap.

A few minutes ago, I heard the garage door open and my father's car pull in. Within moments, my father will open the front door.

BOB BRADLEY

# War Is Hell

A flight of three U.S. Marine F-4U Corsairs came in at wave height and launched a pattern of rockets at the Jap bunker. Offshore the Big Mo and her sister ship, the Wisconsin, rolled with a broadside that rattled over us like a runaway wagon.

My buddy, Lance Corporal Denny Martin, dug his end of the foxhole deeper. Me and Denny had made all of 'em: the Canal, Cape Gloucester, Tarawa, Saipan. Iwo Jima was the worst. For two days the swabs had thrown everything at the Jap positions, but they were still shooting back. A medic carried a wounded G.I. 'reen past us. He didn't look like he'd make it to the hospital ship.

Denny grunted as he tossed more dirt from the foxhole. "Looks like we bought it this time.

Just then, from high on the slopes of Mount Suribatchi, a screeching sound attacked us. "You boys get out of my garden or I will have Mr. Dietret come after you.

Uh-oh, that Jap sounded like a Kraut, a woman Kraut. They were using psychology warfare on us.

Denny dug deeper. "Don't pay any attention to her. She's a German spy."

"Did you boys hear me?" Mrs. Dietret screamed.

I hated to give up our position, but the old bat knew my mother. Mama never was a Marine and didn't like fighting very much. I said, "Better get goin'. Mrs. Dietret is in my Mom's circle at church." I collected my BB gun and water bottle, and trudged toward the fence.

Mrs. Dietret yelled, "I see you there, Burr Hobbs. You fill up that hole or I'll call your mother, and she'll give you what for."

Denny dragged his daddy's shovel and balanced his BB gun on his shoulder. "I bet she's a fanatical German spy who's abducted Mrs. Dietret and is posing as her to get information from us."

"Yeah, like last week at the Scmidleys?" My butt twitched just thinking of the whipping Mama gave me on that one.

Denny knocked mud from his sharpshooter and crawled through the fence. "Was it my fault we got Faustenia's window and she was undressing?"

"Mama didn't see it that way." I cleaned family chicken houses for a month.

Denny said, "You're too sensitive. Where we goin' now?"

His sharpshooter rattled on the cement apron around the Kerrville train station. We tossed our gear on an unguarded dolly.

I wasn't interested in another amphibious landing or another foxhole. I groaned. "This is a dull town."

Denny said, "Yeah, nothing ever happens here."

I nodded vigorously. "I wish we were in the marines in the South Pacific right now, killing Japs." I grabbed my BB gun and mowed down an entire Jap division. Then I sighed and settled back onto the dolly.

War seemed too hard today.

# LYNN BRADLEY

## *The Birthing*

For Lizzie Coleman the time had passed so slowly, especially these last few weeks. But there was so much left to do, and now her chores and plans all had to wait or go unfinished. It could not matter. Not now. Her time had come, and besides, the most important things were done. James had made the cradle. She had boiled the bunting. The cap and stockings she had knitted perfectly matched the christening gown. Next time the Good Reverend Brooks trotted his carriage up their side of the Guadaloupe River, she would be ready.

Lizzie's round abdomen tightened again. It had only been a couple of minutes since the last pain, and each felt stronger than the one before. She stared at the cedar beams crisscrossing the cabin ceiling and gripped the patchwork quilt.

As the pain subsided, she whispered, "Hurry, James, hurry."

She tried to separate the night sounds beyond the cabin: the river gurgling around a fat limestone rock, crickets chirping to their mates, a whip-o-will chanting its call. Were those hoof beats rushing across the clearing. No, she decided, only the wind galloping through the sycamores.

The next contraction shut out all sound but her own. The scream escaped from where it had grown for months, months of wondering if she were one of the "natural birthers" she had heard older women discuss in quiet tones. Or would she die birthing her first born? Lizzie lay back on the feather pillow, her damp hair clinging to her scalp, her thoughts begging for James.

The pendulum clock ticked relentlessly. Then muscles squeezed her belly toward her backbone and took her breath away. Lizzie pulled the edge of the quilt to her mouth and bit hard, muffling the cry as her body demanded she push. "Mama, why didn't you tell me it was so hurtful?" she cried to the empty room.

James dismounted as his horse pushed dirt into puddles at the rail. "She's coming, Lizzie! Miz Margaret's coming!" he shouted.

The horse pulling Margaret McHaney's wagon cleared the cedar break fifty yards away about the time James bounded across the dog run between the kitchen and cabin. He raced toward the bedroom and jerked aside the dividing curtain.

Lizzie, a small bundle beside her, smiled up at him from the bed. "Guess I'm just a natural birther, James. Say hello to your daughter?"

# Red, White, and Black

After World War II, people celebrated life. Even Mothers' Day festivities were grand occasions. Brilliant buffets, soft sounds of pianos, and rose corsages, red or white. Red revealed that one's mother still lived, while white disclosed her death. A story told simply, through the color of a rose.

Six years after the War, after her dad shed his uniform and her mother shed her dad, a white florist's truck stopped at the little girl's house. A delivery man, armed with a box for long stemmed roses, adjusted a fiery red ribbon that surrounded the box and rang the doorbell. Unaware, perhaps, he handed the child Pandora's box.

In her dad's familiar flowing script, her mother's name rested on the outside of an empty envelope. The little girl, the unintended recipient, slipped the shiny ribbon down the length of the box. As it circled her wrist, the richness of satin, new to her childish skin, distracted her curiosity as she rubbed the ribbon bracelet along her arm.

Her mother pried the box from the child's grasp before she could protest. Carefully, not to damage the roses inside, the woman lifted a layer of waxy green tissue that hid them. Upon seeing the contents of the box, her mother dropped it and fled, leaving the child to gather the crunchy bundle of dead black roses from the floor and ponder the story being told, through the color of a rose.

JUDY BRAND

# *Dream Child*

When I saw her in my dreams, she looked like an image that
had stepped from an aging black and white photograph. A
sepia toned photograph, whose blacks and whites and grays
had been warmed by a coating of brown. Yet, the cold reality
of the photo endured. A child, perhaps two years old, wore a
hand-smocked dress of a light tone, almost white. Her shoulder
length hair was a light to medium tone, blonde perhaps. The
tattered teddy bear in her arms had dark, possibly brown, fur.
The dream narrator hinted that I knew the child, that she
needed my help. Each time I saw her sitting on the street
curb, I wanted to run to her, hold her, and protect her from the
unknown. I thought she was my daughter whenever she
appeared. Yet, I knew she was not. The dream narrator implied
that the identity of the child was a significant issue. The child
appeared repeatedly and when she did, I failed to recognize
her. I awoke with a lingering frustration that accompanied
me throughout the day. Then, the apparition began to haunt
my daylight hours. Who was this child in black and white,
dusted in shades of gray, I wondered. The helpless little girl
made my heart hurt when she entered my mind. On the night
that I discovered her identity, my mind was as clear as the
sky illuminated by the fullness of the harvest moon. Sleep
came easily and quickly erased the day's remaining thoughts.
I was relaxed and receptive to the proposals of the narrator of
dreams. Hearing the revelation itself was like once again
learning the answer to a long forgotten riddle. I was surprised,
initially, but not shocked when the narrator announced that I
was the abandoned child in my dreams.

## MARTHA EVERHART BRANIFF

# If I Laid You Down

**I** would fly with blackbirds on the day of your dying and place ten thousand stones around your head, then hold your hand while mourners oiled and washed your body before I laid you down. Or I would sculpt the finest urn to hold your ashes and burn your body on a pyre, a sacrifice to futile gods, then scatter your holy dust over fields where I once laughed at your pollen-yellow nose smelling every flower.

If I laid your bones, cleansed by sun and wind and earth, and kissed your passing, I would cry a heart-pierced lament, a requiem for your spirit wrenched from my soul, the caverns of my body infused with running grief, imbued with thorny pain.

I would lie on your grave, longing for the smell of you and for a final taste of your dripping refreshment: a cool summer stream never to pass my lips again.

MARTHA EVERHART BRANIFF

# Adolph and Jeanie: A Love Story

Hair awry, ten scraggly teenagers with unbalanced postures
and fiery eyes, dodged cars and trailed across a busy street
toward the fine arts museum. The doormen had been warned,
but they stared anyway, aghast at the sight of this unkempt
and rowdy group from a local psych hospital. But Van Gogh,
no doubt, was smiling at the schizophrenics and junkies who'd
come to view works of famous madmen.

Before entering the museum, they loitered on the
sidewalk and drew last puffs from their cigarettes. Young
Adolph, lisping and painfully thin with bulging eyes and a
neck like the Christmas goose, scrutinized the scene. Fresh
from the locked ward, he wore a starched waitress uniform,
pocket stuffed with a pink lace handkerchief, and had
completed his ensemble with black glossy pumps.

He languidly blew smoke rings into the faces of Degas'
life-sized stone dancers, then flipped his cigarette butt under
their graceful legs. An indignant guard demanded he retrieve
the fuming debris, so Adolph crawled between the statue's
pointed toes. The sight of him caused the others to snicker:
his scrawny hairless legs topped with a splash of lime green,
tie-dyed bikinis.

While the patients formed a half circle and listened to
a guard drone on about museum rules, Jeannie slipped in
beside Adolph, gazing at him with rapt attention. Tall and
slender, almond eyes and mocha skin, Jeannie could have
been a model for *Seventeen;* except she didn't talk in any
language one could understand. Most days she didn't utter a
word. Her voice, when she unexpectedly made a sound, was
a monotone of garbled syllables in the constrained timbre of

53

a child who has cleft palate. But Jeannie's palate was normal, and her quick darting eyes took in the world. Rumor spread among the patients that her parents had spent thousands, searching for a reason for her condition.

The disheveled group shuffled from gallery to gallery until they reached an arresting canvas, "The Scream" by Edvard Munch. They clustered around Adolph who stood closest to the painting and pointed to the figure's wide frightened eyes and splayed fingers lifted to its cheeks in horror. He said the painting reminded him of the reaction of several guests at a party he'd attended, when he and a friend had attempted sexy things on the dining table.

The guards followed closely after that.

Fascinated with Francisco Goya's graphic etchings, Adolph lingered in the room filled with the artist's depictions of war. Seemingly a prisoner of the gruesome images, Jeanie's eyes clung to a drawing of a firing squad and she put her face on the glass, leaving smudges of forehead, nose and lips. Adolph loudly proclaimed Goya would be pleased at her expression of admiration. The guards, however, did not agree and commanded that Jeannie stop kissing the glass. As they left the room, Adolph explained to her how Goya's work was a vivid reminder of his own life in the barrios.

For the rest of the tour, he brooded, mute like Jeannie, until they reached the last gallery in front of a sweeping staircase. Adolph adored stairways. Theatrical and poised, he strode over, ascending midway on the stairs, elevating himself above the others. Enthralled with his antics, Jeanie scrambled up and positioned herself at his feet. Suddenly, Adolph's trill boomeranged off elegant white walls and echoed through adjoining rooms.

"My mouth smells like a toilet."

Complete silence fell upon the group before a titter rippled into full-blown laughter. Appalled, the closest docent nabbed Adolph and ushered him into the corner for a terse discussion of protocol.

"That wasn't so bad," someone bellowed. "What about the jerk in Rome who defaced the Pieta?"

Surrounded by guards who had been summoned by the docent, the patients departed from the art museum and returned to the hospital for rest period. Jeannie reclined on her forest green mat in the dayroom, flat on her stomach, cheek to the floor. Her arms and legs bent at elbows and knees were positioned at ninety-degree angles to her body, amphibian style.

"She's part frog," someone laughed, pointing to her position.

"Her parents did this to her," another speculated.

Adolph ceremoniously placed his cherry red mat beside Jeannie, removed his patent pumps and wiggled his toes. When the blinds had been lowered and the lights dimmed, he rubbed her back, leaning so close Jeannie could feel spates of warm breath as he formed syllables against her ear.

"I like you, Jeannie," he said with great affection.

"I like you too," she whispered.

## ELIZABETH BRATTEN

# On the Trail West

The wild gray stallion galloped on, searching for the last grass in drying gulches, filled its belly, and stampeded with the herd to the next canyon. Grizzlies barred the doors of their dens. The winter coats of jackrabbits mimicked the snow. Mountain cats sought shelter in caves below the tree line. The north winds carried the scent of strangers. The wagon train started late, and halted by swollen rivers, circled with Apache raids, and reined in for prayer at trail burials. The wagons rumbled down treacherous inclines led by drivers armed with Winchesters. The eyes of the men are desperate, narrow, and calculating. Each rider searches for a refuge to make camp for the winter. The homesteaders need trees, water, and good ground, where a seed can take root in spring. Inside the Conestoga wagon, a single candle banishes the gloom. The women huddle, keeping warm, taking turns to bolster a dying infant. In the fast-moving dark, winter comes down, and snow. Snow corrals its quarry. Wind and sleet rake the worn canvas sides of the wagon. A blizzard advances the cause of the mountains and shrouds the Overland Trail. Stopped by winter's frozen barricade, the pioneers founder in the charnel house of snow. The moon's bright eye is the witness....

# BILLIE LOU CANTWELL

## Leaving Home

Shadows melt with the dusk. A breeze stirs hovering heat as it whispers through fields. Pickups swoosh along the blacktop and I hear a John Deere strike high gear, heading home.

I sit with Mother on her front porch. The swing squeaks against the rusted chain as I keep it in motion. Mother sits in her rocker as still as the ceramic cat on the top porch step.

"Mother, you know you can't stay out here any longer. The doctor told you didn't he? About the place where they have doctors and nurses to see that you get the therapy you need. He explained to me that your next fall could cause you to break a bone and you couldn't call for help. It's not safe for you way out here alone."

Mother doesn't speak.

A calf bellows in the pasture across the road.

"Sounds like Mr. Marvin has a new calf," I say, to change the subject.

"Mmmhmm. Been hearing it this time every evening." She moves her leg as though to cross it, then sets it down, her soft-soled house shoes make no noise.

The last glow of the sun sinks behind the horizon. How many times has Mother watched this scene? How many times have I? This place holds me, inexplicably, with a tight fist, just as it has held her. Though we share widowhood, I have something else—I lead a busy life. I've just been elected to the city council. I grow restless just thinking about all I have to do.

I walk out into the yard, to the corner of the house. My first memories are of my meanders from this yard, to the well, the barns and the gates to the fields. I can only imagine what memories hover around my mother as she contemplates giving it up.

"What time you plan on leaving in the morning?" she calls. I return to the porch. "Around ten, I guess. I'll come back next weekend and pack up the linens and things. Is there anyone we need to call to tell them you are leaving?"

"No, not that I know of. Don't think anyone will miss me." She rises from her chair and I follow her into the house.

The next morning we are ready to leave by nine, but I keep scurrying around, checking cabinets, the thermostat, the garage doors. I make one more round to be sure the gates are closed before I lock the front door. Mother sits at the kitchen table with her purse and a plastic bag of medicine bottles. She looks impatient and finally speaks with more emotion than I've heard in a long time. "What's keeping you?"

I am hurt by her impatience. Does she understand that her life on this farm is over? I fight back tears as I look around the kitchen. I am giving up my home too. Because I know once my mother walks out the door, home will cease to be here. I know this. Doesn't she?

"Mother, I'm sorry to take you away from here. I don't know what to say to make it easy." Maybe she is acting stoic for me. She shouldn't have to do that. I want her to cry or rave and rant.

She looks at me, frowns, then rises and picks up her purse and medicine. She stops beside the old stove, gives it a little slap and looks at me. "Daughter, don't you know how I've hated that stove? How I've cursed the water that turned every pot I own an ugly orange? How I've hated having to can all those vegetables and wrap all those hogs and calves for freezing that your daddy raised. Don't you know how lonely it's been since he's been gone? Don't you know how I would have given anything to have a close neighbor to gossip with over the fence?"

She walks out, letting the back screen door slam. I follow. She looks at the barns and almost shouts, "Nope, I don't ever have to cook another meal, or call another plumber that won't come. I'm going where somebody else does the worrying. I'll visit with old ladies just like me and raise cane with the hired help, if I'm so inclined." She turned to look back at me. "Come on, Daughter, let's get on to that place where I'm the one who's waited on for a change. Can we stop for a pizza?"

## *From Ocean to Opera*

The couple arrived at the beach while the sun was not yet overhead. He took the oversized umbrella from the trunk on his first trip from the car and secured it firmly in the sand. The lounge chair was placed on the blanket in the umbrella's shade before he came for the picnic basket and her books.

Only then did she emerge from the car. Her long white cover-up hid creamy white skin. A pink, wide-brimmed hat shaded lovely blue eyes from the bright sun. She walked slowly to keep sand from flipping on her heels and getting into her shoes.

Once she was settled he raced to the water, plunging headlong into its splashing surf, letting refreshing coolness sweep over him. He swam far out before letting waves rock him back to shore. Her eyes did not leave his image until she was sure he was within calling distance. Later, on the blanket beside her just out of the umbrella's shade, his cool hand reached to hold hers. He lay in the warm sun with thoughts of his love for the sea and the feel of salt water on his skin. His mind could not imagine a sound more soothing than gentle waves hitting the shore.

They had repeated this scene many times over the past thirty years. He kept these memories close each winter, as he sat patiently in black coat and tie, happy to hold her hand through the long opera that she held so dear.

PAMELYN CASTO

# *Rank Invasion*

In the surprising sun henbit invades my winter yard. Green and lavender, a blanket of nature's tumultuous tossing, cuts a long wide swath through my dormant St. Augustine grass— grass lying in a brown study and which has lost its former smugness. A phalanx of subterranean secrets shouts to my neighbors in green and purple. The lavender flowers, their tubular throats like heralding trumpets, are tiny double-lipped faces, like lewd strumpets, hungry maws. Innocent. The greenery, all scallop-cupped cascading fountains, all calyxes and feathery bracts, has leaves velvety and hairy, veined and finely ribbed as Adam. As animal as I. Unpedigreed Caliban, spawn of hag-seed in wicked morning dew, would have littered the lands with his rank undisciplined kind until chained to his rock—servile, curtailed, and colonized by the crushing spirit of the liberal arts. He could hold no real estate. Liberally, across my backyard, a horde of menacing miracles march— a green and lavender rank invasion knowing how to curse, determined to dream again.

# BETH LYNN CLEGG

## *Family Tree*

**W**ith trembling fingers I open my great-grandmother's small leather coin purse revealing coins from another century, and a note written by my grandmother, a toddler when her mother died in 1881.

"My mother's purse. She earned this quarter by making a dress for our wash woman."

One-hundred-twenty years later, our family tree has branched into a canopy supported by invisible roots. Each generation nurtured by dedicated cultivation of the past. I am now the caretaker of a treasure that makes Mary Ann Todd real.

*Perhaps it was the same for my grandmother.*

*Merry Christmas 2003*

62

BETH LYNN CLEGG   *Bethie*

# *Exit Interview*

You bet I have a comment but move the photographer to my right it's my best side honey I swear I've reached my limit this time you know what I mean after weeks of exhausting rehearsals going over and over every detail of that stupid script never mind my personal sacrifices like dying my hair blonde which turned it to straw and my stylist who I couldn't live without says it'll take months of therapeutic conditioning to reverse the damage now that lying snake-in-the-grass director with absolutely no sensitivity or regard for my feelings after all we shared just announced to the entire cast not in private beforehand mind you that since that awful flood just totally messed up the Arts District and now we're finally getting back to what's important with the reopening two days away he's giving the lead to someone else because I have a slight cold and he's afraid I won't be able to go on like who's going to believe that I mean the reason's so obvious just look at that little tramp clinging to him all lovey-dovey batting those fake eyelashes and the pathetic old fool falling for that phony every-tooth-in-her-mouth-crowned-smile oh she's good I'll give her that more than half his age but twice as smart she knows how to get what she wants but she'll dump him honey he'll be last year's reviews when the play's over and he's no longer useful but if you think I won't teach that lying loser a lesson when he comes crawling back begging for a second chance well guess again still a redhead might be sexier like it could be the real me you know what I mean?

SUZANNE C. COLE

# Spinning

The father blames himself day and night rerunning the ring
road of his limbic system, digging grief grooves. Overriding,
underlying every other experience. Softness of sweet wife
pressed against him frozen in bed by those reckless words.
Autumn colors triumphing in the trees gray in the fog of those
words. Woodsmoke taste of Scotch bitter as the words rise
again like bile. Why aren't words like an errant fishing line?
Aim amiss, hook and fly headed for rotting stump, reel them
back, cast again. No. Once spoken, never called back.

Poring over the power of words—*By thy words thou shalt be
justified, and by thy words thou shalt be condemned.* Judgment
by tongue. As a man speaks so he is. The boy once brought
him a painting of something he'd guessed was a tree. *No,
Daddy,* the boy said, sad-eyed, sad mouth, it's a mountain.
Overhear him later tell the mother, *See my tree?* Mountain
diminished to tree by word alone.

The boy, almost-man, face shiny-tight with pleasure, three
summers' sweat for a Harley Softail, Twin Cam 88 engine,
shotgun duals. Called the color "vivid black." Father's fear
erupting in shrapnel, *That motorcycle will be the death of
you.* Eyes darkening, lip trapped by teeth, son turned away.
Why didn't the father take back those words, tell son his fear,
praise the effort if not the purchase.

Months later slick wet road, spray of gravel, enemy
motorcycle upended, crushed, soft body catapulting off saddle
sliding down road, settling down into posture of sleep, wheel
slowly spinning.

# *Doors*

*An airport elevator door slides open like a theater curtain.
Young black man, face of misery, tall, unnaturally erect,
camouflage dress, combat boots. Wrists shackled, ankles
looped with leg irons, flanked by security guards.*

Etched in memory, that scene. But the young
prisoner's story...can she write it?

On the first floor, wooden shades rattle on the kitchen
door. Door slamming, voice shouting, "Hi, honey, I'm home."
It can't be six already—but a glance at the clock reveals it is.
Frantically, she starts another paragraph:

*A back door slams shut; the breadwinner's home. The
wife shudders as the change in air pressure pushes open her
bedroom door.*

She presses "save," flips off the computer. Nothing
started for supper. No idea of what supper might be. Did she
at least dress this morning? A downward glance confirms
leggings and T-shirt.

"Hi," she calls, "be right there," and rushes to the
bathroom where the mirror reveals she has neglected both
hair and makeup. Combing her hair to the side, she savagely
clips it into place, smears on lipstick. Replaces house shoes
with sandals, emerges to exchange perfunctory hugs with her
husband.

"I'm beat," he says. "What's for dinner?"

"Something yummy, but it'll be a while. How about a
martini?"

"Sounds good."

She hurries downstairs, hauls out gin and vermouth,
measures them into the cocktail shaker, crushes ice, expertly

shakes, then pours into a crystal martini glass. Adds an onion stuffed olive. Carries the drink upstairs on a tray with a small dish of nuts, bumps open the door with her hip. Just settling down to read mail, he barely looks up as she puts down the tray.

"When did you say dinner would be?"

"About seven."

"Good. Remember, I have that board meeting at eight."

She hadn't remembered, and she's pleased. Maybe she can write again after dinner. She doesn't know why, but she's felt compelled all day to write about doors. Returning to the kitchen, she makes her cocktail-tumbler, ice cubes, generous portion of gin, whiff of vermouth. Throwing open the refrigerator, she sees the remainder of the weekend roast. And in the freezer a bag of stir-fry vegetables. Dinner.

*On Saturdays when she was a child, she used to walk with her grandmother to a meat locker in town. Open a heavy steel door and walk into the cold fog, blood-smell oozing from the walls, shrouded shapes hanging from hooks.*

Could opening memory's door become a poem?

Putting on water to boil for rice, she slices an onion and the cold roast lamb.

*Behind that simple door banded in iron and splintering with age is the oldest baptismal font in the United Kingdom. Pushing it open, stumbling on the uneven floor, and wheezing in the dust, they find a rough stone basin, filled with used plastic bags. Silently they exit into a sheep pen, corrugated tin sheets propped up against the church walls. On one an arrow, rivulets of paint descending, points: "The church-this way." Church, sheep pens, lamb, Lamb of God, all who knock (on this door) may enter?*

Dinner preparation goes quickly as she smothers resentment over interrupted writing with a second martini. At seven, she calls him, they eat and drink wine, and he tells her about his day. He does not ask about hers. But he does remind her that his shower stall needs to be de-mildewed, he's left a pair of pants to be hemmed, and she seems to have forgotten his cleaning.

He leaves, and the door slams shut. Rattled, she drinks another glass of wine while cleaning the kitchen.

*A hand holds open the restaurant door for a frail old couple who require a full minute to reach a quiet corner. Carefully they seat themselves on the same side of a booth. Soon a waiter, unasked, brings them a carafe of cool white wine. Carefully the old man pours for both; smiling, they touch glasses.*

What story do they share that she can't hear?

At last she's free to return to her writing. Eagerly, she flips on the monitor, then stares in disbelief at her day's work. Two lines of poetry, three scant paragraphs with three different themes. She tries to shape some of the ideas she had during dinner, but she can't. For an hour she stares at the screen, occasionally writing lines which she immediately deletes.

At ten she turns off the computer and gets ready for bed, but the stories go on.

*A plywood door with cheap locks quickly splinters under the blows of the crowbar. In a back bedroom an old woman clutches a thin quilt to her chest, her heart pounding like a rabbit caught by a dog in a fenced-in yard.*

Maybe she can write it.

Downstairs, the door opens, then slams shut again.

# Love in the Afternoon

**I** was swaying in the porch swing, so lost in my thoughts I didn't see him drive up.

"Emma." His deep voice awoke me from my daydream. A smile spread across my face. Though it was over one hundred degrees outside, he wore jeans and a long sleeved shirt, and his dirty and worn hat partially covered his eyes. I hopped off the swing, bursting to tell him the news.

"I am so glad to see you," I told him. We reached each other and I kissed him. Our lips met delicately and we embraced. I breathed in his rustic outdoors smell and then whispered in his ear how much I loved him. His expression warned me at once that something was not right. Turning his head, he pulled away. Confused, I asked what was wrong.

"It's not you. It's me. I don't deserve you and I don't mean to hurt you," he explained as he backed away, heading toward his truck. I said I did not understand.

"Listen, what we had was not real. What we had was more of a fling than a true relationship. I'm sorry. I can't go through with it." He climbed into the driver's seat and it was then I noticed her. Her brown eyes locked with mine. I'd seen her many times before. He had assured me she was just an old friend, but now she had her arms wrapped around his neck.

"But we are getting married in two weeks!" I cried after him. He threw the truck into reverse. "Buddy! Buddy!" I slipped my ring off of my finger and waved it at him. "Don't leave!" In desperation, I ran after his truck. When I stopped, I was slightly out of breath.

The wind whipped through my hair and I felt particles of sand hitting my face. My eyes teared but not because of the gusts. I stood motionless, shocked with the realization that he was really leaving. I prayed he would look back, but he didn't even glance in the rear view mirror. Aching for his touch, I closed my eyes and imagined his strong arms holding me. Now the sand was stinging my legs but I didn't budge. He had to come back; he didn't understand what he was doing.

I remained there for what seemed hours before emotions flooded over me and I broke down and fell to the ground. How could he do this; how could he leave me?

It was now dusk, and knowing my father would be home soon, I rose and staggered back to the house. At the front steps, I laid my hand on my stomach. "C'mon. It's just you and me now," I said. I opened the screen door and stepped inside. It slammed shut behind me.

# Nurturing

When you become a widow, you realize you never knew what nurturing actually was. Oh, there was the nurturing of others but none for yourself all those years.

You know now that what passed for nurturing from others for you was only their self-interest. Now, when you can no longer matter in their lives, you don't matter.

You're left with yourself, solitary, looking out at the snow, a metaphor for the coldness surrounding you.

"Oh, we'll have to get together when you come to town," says one I once knew. "I'll need a break come spring so I'll be up to see you," she adds.

Not likely, because I don't answer the phone anymore.

BETTY DAVIS

## *Quandary*

Now that my aunts, uncles, grandparents and parents are dead, now that I am the oldest living person in my family, a powerful place, a place of fear, the sun still rises like it does not know, does not feel my quandary and the wind still rubs my nerves, massages their degeneration like it expects the usual expression of joy.

The cliff I am on confuses me. On one end, I want to go, to fly on the air currents until I find where my ancestors live. On the other, I hunker against cold rock, hiding from a future that may not be what I expect. Hiding fails me as life pulls me down road where rising, dressing, eating leaves the cold rock behind and forgotten.

Though the future pushes me into games, computers and all things in the pot of technology, I must not forget my friend, the goal of my life, to love, to live, to write, to publish, and to worship the giver of a life I would not give back.

Now that I remember what I must do, I ponder the path ahead. The lane narrows and dims until distant mystery gathers up the experiences I have yet to know. I am grateful the guard at the gate of the future stands firm, ready to surprise me each day with a turn of the key.

# The Way of the Thin

The time has come when the scale shows I have lost ten pounds by starving. Today I am binging. Bread and jelly, three bananas, four tablespoons of peanut butter, bread and butter, boiled ham, provolone three slices. This is what I have eaten between breakfast and lunch.

The binging was as predictable as my sneezes in the fall. I tell myself I deserve a day of eating, a reward. It turns into two days and two weeks and the ten pounds I lost in two months is back. Discouragement is waiting there on the edge of the fat, it's cue a fertile seedpod ready to erupt. Staying in bed all day, I allow the fat cells to swell without resistance. I know I cannot lose the weight before summer when I put on a swimsuit that reveals to the world what a glutton I am.

The next day I slog to the kitchen in my bathrobe, make coffee. I will fast this morning, try to starve my depression and desperation, to punish myself for failure. While the coffee brews, I turn on the TV.

"It's not your fault," a plump, sad-faced man says. "You aren't alone." He tells me where to get help.

I decide to call the clinic that promises at least company for my obesity. They suggest a support group and I agree to go to Over Eater's Anonymous which meets at my church every Thursday.

The first meeting I wear a too-large dress so I look like I am smaller than I used to be. First glance from my collective peers tells me I can do nothing to successfully deceive them. I want to run backwards from this group of "happy hungries," but something in their relatedness holds me fast. If I can just drop my deceiver's mask and present the fat facts, maybe just maybe, I can duel with the scale on equal terms.

Less than enthusiastic about admitting my compulsion to these strangers, I surprise myself when they call on me, buck up and do it. It feels better than I expected. I have been on the defensive so long I did not consciously remember it is all right to admit I eat too much, that I lack self-control in this area. After all, it is not like I am a total failure. Before I finish talking, I have revealed to them I am an accomplished musician, a successful tax accountant, a good mother, have a happy marriage, am patriotic, work in my church, visit the sick and more. So I have one problem I have to work on, that is not so bad.

The group seems a tad less intimidating by the time we are half way through the meeting. I am feeling a warmth grow inside me, as if I have come home from a long absence in the cold. This group is suddenly very important to me, like a family. My other family has supported my fat for years, and I become aware this new family will support me in another way, the way of the thin.

We shake hands, hug and smile each other back to the world of polite reassurances and phony affirmations given us by the thin ones who never had a fat person on their outside. As I leave, the thin person inside me jumps up and clicks her heels together as joyfully as if she had just bought a new Toyota and could fit into it.

# PAULINE M. DELANEY

## *Bait*

We leave our sheltered valley this bleak November day for one last mountain climb. We hike through fields of asters burned by cold, past fireweed drooped with frost. We step aside to let a truck and trailer pass. A swayback mare, her nostrils flared, her eyes white-rimmed with fear, stares through the trailer slats. Her bony sides are heaving. Too old to work, too old to foal, she seems to know this journey is her last, that in a nearby mountain glade she'll be goaded from the trailer, tethered to a tree. To wait.

No one needs a work-worn mare. And hunters pay good money to kill a bear.

## CANDACE DIMITRI

# *Homily for Halloween*

**I** mark my house, taping to windows a cardboard skeleton, limbs contorted into the lotus position, my daughter's construction paper pumpkin, grinning its 28th annual greeting, and a faded black cat created by my son at five to cross no one's path.

When I was five, Aunt Martha in witch's disguise stuck her head out her darkened door and scared me so good I swallowed my scream. That scream hid within my growing body until its unexpected, embarrassing escape years later when I first viewed death lying unmasked in Aunt Martha's coffin.

More familiar now with death, I am able to watch as a neighbor's black cat, not mindful of my attempts to delay the inevitable, waits at the base of bird-bearing trees for prey to fall. I have seen this lesser deity bat at and roll back and forth on top of the vulnerable. I can't resist returning to the window, hoping that the game is over.

With my offerings individually wrapped, I wait in a doorway, brightly lit, revealing my gray and wrinkles not false faced. On this Allhallows Eve, I treat myself to a child's expectation, a fantastic procession of powerful super heroes and protected princesses whose parents have costumed control.

WENDY DIMMETTE

# When You Climb a Mountain

These mountains are old as the wind and salt of a sea floor that ground them up and left them in layers of limestone and waves of wind and water, pressed them the way stars are pressed in the condensed darkness of evolution and upheaval. Halfway to the top I stand still and let the mountains move. I feel the rush of slow-motioned valleys taking in rock and mudslide to spread them precisely and forever in Geology, and the hush covering a plan that does not deviate. Eons beneath my feet remnants of an ancient ocean escape on underground rivers whose force clefts peaks along fault lines I can't see. Slopes that seem random are not. They're an exactitude of tectonics where pieces like countries rub against each other. Where species like armies fight for space. And where each of us reach from the shoulders of those who brought us this far. My climb counts. It's where I stand in the history these mountains keep like chapters in a book. And it changes everything: by breaths that deepen fernshade and leafmold, by thoughts that hover above blossoms hybridized by footprints I couldn't stop. Even from here I can see that whatever it is I am becoming will claw itself up the cold face of granite until altitude wrings me out and the dust that tints my shadow takes it back.

MARK A. EVANS

# Chicken Day on Papa's Farm

Cold streaks of sky slice gray and hazy trapping winter sun from view—just another Amarillo Thanksgiving coming soon. Though winter scuffles its feet behind autumn the chill in the air causes faint fog to form when Papa talks.

"Your Granny wants chicken for dinner." He pauses as he stokes the fire brewing in the open barrel where they burn things. You want to help?"

The flames begin to shoot up as if somehow the fire knows it is chicken day—as if the barrel, the flame, and the winter sky conspire with death hovering in the air.

I can't look Papa in the face when I answer, "No, Papa. I don't want to help." And I run to Granny's side, where she stands on the porch waiting to lend a hand to Papa.

"Go inside, young'n," she says and pats my behind lightly. "Scoot."

I hurry inside the warm familiar house that will cloak me from seeing death (and Papa and Granny wringing chicken necks). I sit facing opposite the window, hiding and listening to the howl of the early afternoon wind slapping the window, half-covering the sounds of Granny and Papa talking.

"He's only nine, Claud."

"That boy seems scared of everything, Hazel." The wind tackles the house louder; Papa and Granny's voices are drowned out.

Suddenly I hear a shriek, and Papa yells, "Well, Hazel!" I jump around and sit high on my knees, surprised at the sight outside. On the two sets of clotheslines in the backyard, chickens all in a row, are hanging by their feet. Some are squawking, wings flapping frantically; some have necks hanging limply; others are headless. I look for Granny among the line-up and see her chasing one of the headless chickens that has come untied. It looks like a game of tag, with Granny running after that chicken.

The chicken runs around like it knows where it's going. It jerks wildly and runs through the back gate into the open field toward the barn where it falls, jerks again, and finally lays motionless. Granny stands over it, her brow tight, mouth grimaced, and she is breathing hard from all that running. I am so shaken at seeing all of this. At the same time tears trickle from my eyes, Papa sees me staring in disbelief out the window. The next thing I remember, Granny is hugging me tightly in her arms, and I feel queasy and dizzy.

Thirty years later, I walk across the barren back yard. Two clothesline poles stand guard over the nothingness. The wind blows and a chill works its way from my back to my neck. I look to where the gate used to be, and notice the two large barrels that were used for burning things. I pull my jacket closer to me, stuffing my hands deep into the pockets. The clotheslines have been gone for some time now. They disappeared not long after Granny and Papa died. After all these years I still visit the old farm from time to time, just to remind me about them. This house, this yard, this farm were all such a part of them. Even now, though, I struggle to hold good thoughts of Papa and Granny to my heart. My body trembles and another shudder escapes from within me; the first thing I always picture is those damn chickens hanging in two rows, while death conspires with the flames from the barrels where they burn things.

# *Eclipse*

"**B**e careful, son," she whispered as she stood on her porch and watched the sky-blue pickup fade into the distance. A candle was lit and a prayer was said for his safe return. By fate, tires grazed gravel. Life disappeared in a golden field of wheat. For the repose of his soul, she burned one last candle. Staring at the flickering flame of eternity, she drifted into darkness.

# YOLANDA FALCON

## *Stardust*

The cab driver honked the horn as he pulled up to the small gray brick house on Mulberry Street. After a few minutes, Benny came out the front door, gripping the wood-carved cane he bought on one of his jaunts to the border.

Benny was known for his Saturday night ritual of carousing until sunrise. Most people thought he was single by the way he carried on with the ladies. He claimed he was born with an outgoing personality over which he had no control. After fifty long years of marriage, his wife simply accepted him as is.

Those who knew Benny could bet on where he was going when he wore his heavy starched blue jeans, and long-sleeved white shirt with the pearl snap-buttons.

"Take me to the Stardust Bar," he said as he got into the taxi.

He was going to meet a drinking buddy he hadn't seen in a long time. Reminiscing with the cab driver about his youthful escapades seemed to rejuvenate Benny's spirit. Anxious to get to his favorite honky-tonk, he ordered the driver to step on the accelerator.

"I've been cooped-up too long," declared seventy-nine-year-old Benny. "It's time to get back into the swing of life."

When he arrived at the bar, Benny pulled a roll of money from his pocket, mostly one-dollar bills, which he used to pay for his fare.

The flashing yellow neon sign, *Open till 2:00 a.m.,* brought back memories that made him grin. As he entered the crowded lounge, he had gained a little strut in his step.

Benny was back to his old ways.

Jesse was there just as he expected, as were a few others he knew. After the usual handshaking and pats on the back, they ordered a round of beer. Benny embraced the bottle as he slowly raised it to his lips.

"Carmen's been sick, so I've been staying home to take care of her," Benny said. "I just needed to get out of the house for awhile. Her constant nagging is driving me crazy."

"You mean to tell me Carmen hasn't had the sense to divorce you by now?" Jesse laughed.

"She'd never leave me."

"Don't be so sure about that. And how's your son?"

"Eddie's fine. He's in the Army."

"Army? I thought he was a mechanic."

"He is...of course he is," Benny said as he stared at the people on the dance floor.

It didn't take Benny long before he noticed the tawdry middle-aged woman sitting at the bar. She was wearing a low-cut peacock-blue dress, two sizes too small. Her auburn hair needed taming as much as she did.

Just as Benny was thinking about approaching the woman, his son walked in.

Eddie's face turned beet-red when he saw his father.

"Pop, you had me worried. I've been looking for you since I got off work."

"Since when did you become my keeper?" Benny frowned. "Pull-up a chair and have a beer. A night out might do you some good."

"Good to see you, Eddie," Jesse said as he shook Eddie's hand.

"Did your mother send you here?" Benny asked. "I swear that woman would keep me on damned leash if she could."

In a stern voice, Eddie said, "Time to leave, Pop." Then, he took his father by the arm and helped him off the barstool.

"Don't be a stranger and let another year go by before I hear from you again," Jesse said with a sense of sadness. "At our age, we can't ever be sure of tomorrow. By the way, be sure to say hello to Carmen."

Eddie turned to Jesse in utter surprise and said, "I thought you knew...my mother died about six months ago."

What Benny had forgotten, he now struggled to remember, as the jukebox played unfamiliar songs. His only comfort now was the music he carried within his heart.

At the door, Benny turned to wink at the temptress in blue, and raised his Aztec painted cane as if to propose a farewell toast. Then, he quietly departed into the pale moon night.

# *Appassionato*

**W**ide plank floors sank under my saddle oxfords as they clanked into Mrs. Peacock's School of Piano. Swallowed up in the smell of ancient varnish and musty music books, I waited on the wobbly wooden bench until time for my lesson to begin. Mrs. Peacock, a barrel-shaped woman with a trumpet voice, always wore a dress with small flowers with a thin belt cinching her waist. I wondered what shape the barrel would take were the belt to be relieved of its duty.

"Mr. Yuri is ready for you now," she heralded, her voice unrationed.

He sat on the bench at the long-as-a-mile piano. If he had expected a prodigious wonder, his hopes vanished as I blundered through the simplified Chopin score. He corrected hand and finger positions and pointed out missed crescendos and pianissimos with rolling pedantic rhythm—but no passion.

I wanted passion! I was sure he had it—he was from Russia, and I was certain everyone from Russia was very passionate—about everything. His mask of indifference served as fuel for my ravenous heart as it preyed upon his psyche for any glimmer of zeal that might escape. Ever watchful, I was prepared to catch it in a flash—it would be like the train of cometic light—brilliant, white and red ribbon of blaze that I would ride into the black gaze of his eyes in search of the nucleus of his fervor.

Mrs. Peacock remained at her desk in the hall. Dutifully, I gave her the envelope my mother had charged me to deliver. A fat little hand came forth from the barrel of flowered apparel, and she smiled, grabbing it wildly. In the thick ledger resting in the middle of her desk, she recorded the transaction, perfectly, *con molto appassionato!*

## CAROLYN TOURNEY FLOREK

# *Quarry Walk*

I was twelve when I walked to an abandoned limestone quarry along a farm road paved in mud and crushed stone. Crescent hoof-prints of an unshod horse pointed like arrows for me to follow down this rarely traveled road. When I came to the quarry's edge I looked down and noticed a small lake rimmed with ice. From above I could see all of winter's nakedness reflected in the glassy water. Large elliptical fish drifted just below the surface. I wanted a closer look so I went down along the quarry's rim to the place where trucks once waited to be filled with rock. I walked into the brush and boulders along the edge and then carefully stepped onto the ice ledge. I saw the fish, their silvery scales—ice crystals encasing their motionless bodies in secret hibernation. My focus in water moved to the reflection of trees—a tangle of dark veins netting the suspended fish. I went back to the bank for a rock or something to throw at the fish. I found a long stick, returned to the ice, and held the stick like a spear over the water. I saw myself in the mesh of branches, my face with the fish in their cold and bloodless world beneath the surface. I became aware of the ice giving way and lunged at a boulder half in the water. I clung to the rock and pulled myself up. Ice had broken away and was floating over where the fish had been.

Later, in the evening, it began to snow. I watched snowflakes by streetlight and hoped for no school. Soon the road would be covered and the lake completely frozen.

DEBORAH FRONTIERA

# Hoarfrost and Rose Petals

I wanted Mom to see it—the fairy wand of sun streaking through the February fog in Rochester, Minnesota. I guided her arm, patient with her deliberate steps and short breaths, to the fifth story hall window near the cardiac unit. Arms around each other, we drank in the scene. Sun sparkled diamonds to the twig tips of every tree. Back in her room, Daddy handed me coffee. They were ready for her in surgery. Hours dragged. Sun climbed the sky, melted the frost into gray limbs, the street to mud and slush, then set again umteen games of cribbage later. Dark turned slush to dirty ice. "I'm sorry," the nurse said to my father, "your wife passed away during surgery." We staggered across the street for a double vodka martini—up with a twist—a glass of wine, and two grilled sandwiches with no taste. Fog rolled into our minds, through the necessary arrangements, and settled over the drive home ahead of the next blizzard—the blizzard that would strand the rest of the family at the Detroit and Minneapolis airports to make even longer drives in rented cars on icy roads. But sparkles filled a clear night sky our last evening together— fireworks. "Give her a good send off," my brother said. Four months later we gathered again, wearing winter coats in June for the late spring chill on Lake Superior. Middle-aged children sprinkled ashes, young adult grandchildren scattered rose petals while the newest generation smiled. The sun stretched her fairy wand through the clouds, sparkled off the petals. If I close my eyes, I can still see the sun on the hoarfrost and the rose petals, feel her last hug of joy in the beauty of simple things.

# MARCIA GERHARDT

## *Wings*

In the country, my father has a duck pond filled with water from engines pumping daily to keep the level high in the cavernous hole, almost two acres wide. Ready for his mallards, my father visits the duck man. I help pick out the most stunning of the bunch. He has a bright, golden beak and the duck man nods his approval at my choice.

Beautiful specimens, father has their wings clipped so they will stay on the pond he built for them...all of them, even my duck. At night before I sleep, I imagine his loss, then dream. Father is sawing away at my limbs so I won't leave.

They glide majestic, a pretty site, pretty enough to paint. Mother sits by the pond's edge, her paintbrush waving benedictions on canvas. She fills our house with pictures of ducks, swimming, quacking, dipping mustard beaks in the controlled water level of the pond.

My parents go every day to watch their shimmering blue necks, banded in white, stretch in anticipation, as they follow my father who walks slowly, teasingly around the pond's edge, duck food clutched in his fists.

One day they visit the pond and there are no ducks, only feathered debris abandoned by the fox.

Years later, my mother presses a china mallard in my hands. Your father would want you to have this, she says.

The duck shimmers in my fingers as I hold it against the light and I am reminded of what can happen when you clip wings from living things.

J. LEE GOODMAN

# White Water

Under the flaming ball of gas hanging low on the horizon, she appeard placid. Shadows disguised her true design, and her swollen folds beckoned, *Navigate me.* With a sudden northern gust, treacherous lapping waves echoed from shore to shore, *Forward canoe,* but the pulsing current forced retreat to calm water. *Come,* she cried, as white foam teased the paddle, daring excitement, challenging satisfaction. Serenity dulled my senses as I plunged into the void. Smooth canyon walls engulfed my vessel, rocking and gliding upon a fluid path. Deeper the paddle thrusts into the depths, reaching and pulling against the stream. Pooling sweat trickled from the effort and every muscle strained. My mind reeled, precious energy spent—white water lies ahead.

J. LEE GOODMAN

## *The Changing Face*

I sensed "the eyes" following me as I walked toward the bookstore, and hastened my long gliding strides. Someone was lurking, undressing my form, but I didn't mind the unwonted feeling. I savored it.

My schedule was leisurely, and I spent the morning fastidiously grooming. I enhanced the warm water of my bath with a handful of sea salt, and the slippery feeling it created on my skin stirred a hidden passion. The brackish taste on my arm invoked memories of afternoons at the beach and snorkeling on the reef. Surrounded by warmth, I reclined against the white porcelain, and listened to the ripples generated by my hands. I could afford this calming luxury now.

I got out of the tub, minutes before shriveling, surrounded myself in thick terry and briskly toweled dry. A slathering of body lotion completed the ritual, and I painted my toenails a subdued red, arranged my hair and applied make-up. The silky under dressings I slipped over my body shimmered in the pink glow of my boudoir. The years have been good to me I thought, assessing the figure in the mirror. There were a few unsightly curves that didn't survive the firmness of youth, several silver threads among golden locks, and lines decorated my face from many character phases, but I felt alluring. Finally after years of recrimination, I had confidence. I planned to walk today, but I wore the sexy sandals anyway. They looked best with my flowing crimson dress.

"The eyes" were burning my skin, and my dress offered no shield from the heat. Ducking into the bookstore,

I purchased the book of poetry I ordered, and decided to read a few passages at the sidewalk café next door. The white tablecloth reflected a clean light onto the pages and the familiar words settled into my heart. Familiarity had not quenched the emotion that still overwhelmed me. Sweet creamed coffee sated the bitterness as a tear trickled down my cheek. Where is my knight?

Unexpectedly, a masculine voice asking to share my table broke my reverie. I blocked the sun and looked up. It was his eyes that had been watching me, sensitive blue pools, not the piercing flames I imagined. His tall shadow spread over the table, and the sudden temperature change slowed my racing pulse. The ensuring friendly banter eased my fear, and I offered him the vacant chair. He noticed my book of poetry, and related a favorite of his own. He was easy to talk with and conversation flowed steadily from his full lips. I felt shallow as I reviewed the physical aspects of his person. Fine features framed with thick dark hair, svelte physique; he was a feast to the eye. He ordered black coffee and we chatted for hours. His rapier wit enchanted me and I laughed freely. Absorbed in our shared dialogue, I hesitated to look at my watch. It must be almost noon, and I had an important date. He suggested we have lunch at the French bistro across the art museum, but I said no. I have an engagement at noon; please excuse me. I got up to leave, and he asked, tomorrow? My heart skipped to think that he had an interest in me. Yes, tomorrow at the bistro and I floated out of his view.

Spring's renewal surged through my body and fragrant pink cherry blossoms and lavender hyacinths filled my senses as I hurried down the cobbled walk. Three blocks and I was standing in front of a brownstone, blushing. I felt like an ingénue. I reached for the bell, and the door opened to a melodic chorus...Grandma!

JOHN GORMAN

# *February: Cold Front: Houston*

The wind is in the street that's finally been built high enough
with three-story, five-story motels and office cubes to seem a
place, a canyon raised on the prairie. The sky is serious. *I
could snow,* it says. *We could crack,* say cypress and sweet
gum, *we need not come to leaf.* The palms rattle long fronds.
The traffic doesn't listen, though a few cars and vans have
their lights on now in midafternoon. The traffic can't care
that the neon on the new fancy-ish restaurants has acquired a
sudden poignancy, as in grainy pictures of places with
discontinued treatments of milk-fed capon on the menu,
passenger pigeon pasties, Nesselrode Pie. To our south, almost
in Mexico, holes open in bridges, cars drive out over them
and fall. Three drivers, six, gone to death in the water. The
wind can't care as it worries the brightgreen grass, the hired
landscaping. A fat man with a plastic bag of cans struggles
with his sports cap. A woman with a flat box of donuts
demonstrates aerodynamic principles. The trees, the awnings,
go crazy. *Nothing lasts,* the wind says—though I'll bet the
year is warming with new fosterage, I'll bet we're about to
see thirty times the flowers. And what is the wind, compared
to an Aussiestyle steak house, a transmission repair center,
an assisted living facility with a lovely 18th Century cupola?
The wind is nothing Platonic. It's a bluster, a series of gusts.
*None of this stuff,* the wind says, *including your insights, will
last.*

## NANCY GUSTAFSON

# *Full Moon Undraped*

Sleepless the night before her wedding, she lies for the last time in her familiar room, on her cozy bed, warm beneath her quilt; the unforeseeable is a smoldering ember. Rising in the east, a full moon undraped. Tomorrow the transition: wife, on a different bed, beneath another quilt, dawn in an unfamiliar room. She hears her father climb the stairs. Worn slippers mark each step; his shadow fills the doorway. For the last time in her familiar room he kneels beside the bed and prays for her. Peace shatters fear, blankets her in eiderdown counterpane; faith is a glowing ember. She sleeps.

NANCY GUSTAFSON

# Lunch With Aunt Biddy

Taking her ninty-year-old Aunt Biddy to lunch was one of those January responsibilities that Maxine dreaded. But here they were again, in Luby's Cafeteria.

"We might as well begin our yearly ritual, Aunt Biddy. What was the best thing that happened to you last year?"

Aunt Biddy fingered the strands of multicolored plastic beads that hung around her neck.

"It was a wonderful year, but I think the best of all was going to Mardi Gras. A clown on stilts was throwing beads into the crowd—free, no charge! I really scrambled to get these beads. Fell over and nearly got squashed like a toad on the road. Lady Godiva picked me up."

"Most people hang those plastic beads from their rearview mirrors, Aunt Biddy," Maxine criticized.

"Sure enough? That seems like a waste, to me. Besides, I hardly ever drive my car anymore."

Aunt Biddy popped several pieces of fried okra into her mouth, then squirreled them into her cheeks so that she could talk.

"Your turn, Honey. What was the best thing that happened to you last year?"

Maxine rolled her eyes, embarrassed at her aunt's too-loud voice and lack of proper table manners.

"It's hard to say, Aunt Biddy. It was a very bad year, with the divorce and all. I suppose the best was going with the Galveston Lady's Society to see Janacek's *Katya Kabanova* at the Wortham Center. But our seats were so high up we couldn't see a thing, and I was dizzy through the whole performance."

"Well, I swan. I wish you'd had better seats." Aunt Biddy knitted her brow in sympathy. "What's the worst thing that happened to you, Honey?"

"Our trip to Ireland. George insisted we go. Said it would help our relationship, but it just made things worse. For one thing, all the food tasted like peat. They dig it right out of the bogs and cook with it. Nasty! They drive on the wrong side of the road, and that caused us to have our little wreck. I ordered a complete set of Belleek china, but by the time it arrived in Galveston, the sugar bowl was chipped."

"Of all the bad luck! You've really had a time of it this year, Sweetheart."

Aunt Biddy drew Maxine's hand to her lips and kissed it. Maxine glanced around the restaurant, then wiped her hand on her napkin.

"That's enough of my problems, Aunt Biddy. Tell me the worst thing that happened to you last year."

Aunt Biddy took a bite of fried chicken, and with grease dribbling down her chin, related a story leading to the worst thing that happened last year.

"Back in seventy-five, I was making Jack an apple pie and didn't have enough apples. So I looked through the cupboard and spied a jar of pears. I mixed them with the apples, and Voila! I had invented pear-apple pie. Then I made a terrible mistake! *Fool that I am*, I went to the Piggly Wiggly next day and blab-blab-blabbed to everybody I saw. Told that checkout girl my recipe in detail. In the March two thousand and one *Woman's World* that recipe was printed. Someone in that Piggly Wiggly stole my recipe, bided her time so I couldn't sue, and then sold it to the magazine and got rich on my invention. If Jack were alive, he'd be outraged!"

Maxine was relieved when Aunt Biddy finally finished eating. The best-and-worst game was over until next January, and Maxine could report to her Sunday School class that she had performed a kindness to a pixilated old woman.

Aunt Biddy's head blazed a trail to the cashier's stand, her Mardi Gras beads swinging like rosaries from a rearview mirror. She navigated between tables, proud to show off her niece.

"Thank you so much, Honey. You're too good to me. I hope this year is better for you. Do you have anything you're looking forward to?"

"Not a thing. It appears another dismal year is in store for me. What do you have to look forward to, Aunt Biddy?"

Aunt Biddy's eyes sparkled with mischief. She jingled her beads and giggled like a little girl about to open her birthday present.

"This year at Mardi Gras, I'm going to get the big beads."

JOYCE POUNDS HARDY

# The Funeral

She had never been so angry. They did not even speak the same language, how were they ever going to solve their problems. She poured her heart out day after day, her emotions raw, needing to be said, needing to be excavated from the caverns of pain, needing to be heard. But no! The monstrous ego pretended to listen to every word, pretended to forgive her ignorance, her mistakes, her apologies. She believed, naively, that her feelings were falling on an understanding heart, that there was some sympathy glowing in those cold eyes. But she was wrong. It hurt to discover that it was a charade; she knew now that that cruel ego did not give a damn about what she was experiencing, what she was trying to say. For her, the light just went out; it just snapped. It was as if that monster did not have any sensitivity; and suddenly, she knew for sure that there wasn't. She contemplated suicide. She contemplated revenge. Better yet, murder. She found a claw hammer that workmen had left outside her apartment door. Without a second thought, she calmly walked into the room and caught his Majesty sleeping as usual. With a smile on her face, she bashed and bashed and bashed until the monster quivered and died. She held the funeral on Re-boot Hill, a grand affair in the newest section of *Pere LaChaise*. No one blamed her for her outrage; in fact, they cheered her. Everyone came and threw old disks and burned-out modems, outdated programs and warped CD-ROMS on the fresh dirt. Relatives came by the dozens, the Apples and the Macintoshes, the Hewlett-Packards and the Dells, taking note of the assembled anger. They decided among themselves to be kinder in the future, lest there be more raving lunatics lurking in the guise of a lovable, innocent-looking little old lady, who even now was dancing on their cousin Compaq's grave.

95

## JOHN HAYMAKER

# The Slide

**M**aarten had taken his five-year-old daughter, Jena, to their weekend outing in the park. She often coaxed him to swing along with her, but Maarten would stand behind her like the other dads, each gently pushing their child in a swing. Today, he gave a running push to the merry-go-round, then watched as his daughter sat on the iron bars, giggling for all the world, her golden pony tail swinging freely in the wind. Round and round she went until she bounded off the still-spinning go-round and went running for the giant slipper-slide, a marvelous corkscrew slide covered over by a riveted steel enclosure.

Maarten followed behind his daughter and held his hands on her shoulders as they waited in line. When Jena's turn came, he helped her up the ladder steps, balancing her with one hand lightly pressed against her waist until she bravely seated herself at the top of the slide. Maarten pulled her golden hair back with his hands, redoing her ponytail with a blue band, gave her a little kiss and a little push. Her childish screams of delight echoed metallically all the way down. Winded, Jena sat in the sandpit below, leaning back on her hands pressed into sand, laughing with her head thrown back, grinning at her upside-down father. Maarten abruptly grabbed the ladder and climbed up himself. He stood atop the last step, feeling a little foolish as the other fathers looked on.

Screw 'em, he thought, and stood on the very top step, putting one leg in the tube, then the other, positioning himself to ride the giant slide. He grabbed the rim of the tube to give himself a swinging start, and slid down the polished steel. Nearing the first bend of the corkscrew, the tube interior darkened. Momentum forced him to stretch out full length following the contour of the slide, arms at his sides. He could no longer see, but he felt every turn burn his elbows. The turns took him faster and faster. Already dizzy, his head fell backward and banged against the slide. A faint light shone at the end just before he came shooting out in a ball of naked flesh, tumbling along a conveyor belt—a flat mat of individual chrome plates inching forward continuously. Mechanical arms reached out, grabbing him beneath his armpits and stood him upright. All about him he saw thousands more naked forms, exactly like himself. Then another naked form came rolling out of the tube, then another, and yet another. The conveyor belt inched them toward a cap fitter, which was bundling each form in a business suit and ushering them onto a bus. What had happened to childhood, he wondered? What happened to youth? The conveyor belt rattled forward. He turned back to look at the chute opening, and then he started working his way back, bumping into this clone, stepping on the toes of that one, pushing past them all until he was last in line. He climbed atop the tube and straddled it, shimmying upward to find the origins of these clones. Almost reaching the top, he craned his neck to see behind a glass partition a brightly lit room of whirling gizmos and buzzing pumps.

Just then he lost his balance and slid off the chute, falling as if into a bottomless well—falling, falling, helpless, until he tumbled out of the slide onto the sand. A little boy yelled from the top of the slide, "Geronimo!" Jena came running to hug him, giggling, "Oh, daddy, wasn't it fun!" Maarten grabbed his daughter's hand and they ran to line up again.

LINNEA HEANEY

# Autumn Pieced Work

Curved lines scatter like leftover crescents from a teacher's hole punch. Colors of burnt sienna, orange yellow, and red on cotton scraps dropped across the concrete cracks and ridges of stems. Fall rains to dull the oak and maple vibrancy and steal the last warm thoughts of the summer sun seeming to stretch on forever. Rusty leaf patterns stain the sidewalk to grandmother's home. School days are spent ironing gifts of sassafras mittens between melting wax paper with a construction paper frame. Saving a bit of color before shorter days limit the earth to hues of gray. The brisk winter battering frosty chrysanthemums sparks the wondering of how this fleeting time can wear away life to lines of stark trees. Patchwork lines of black and sea green cover grandmother's lap to hold off the first chill. A great grandchild tentatively sits by her side. She leans slowly in to kiss his cheek—and an inner joy eases her back to brief moments. Leaving the home, tears fall. Flannel sheets and faded blue comforter gently hold as the bittersweet call comes that she has passed. Seasons move all forward, hand-stitching a new spring. Quilted emotions cross lines, rising, and falling; remembering a sidewalk of counterpanes, sometimes covered with autumn pieced work.

JAMES HOGGARD

# The River on Us

Skirting sandstone boulders, we reclimbed the hills we'd switchbacked across on our way to the river. We were finally tramping home, and with the edges of our heels we tattooed paths of quarter moons down a dry creekbed, then laid another set across the checkerboard top of a stock tank that was all but dry. Up now on the weedy bank's rise, we were wandering again—no one in a hurry to get to town or home.

Zigzagging mesquite-crowded pasture, we flushed cottontails, lizards and finches and a long rat snake. We made a labyrinthine way through short walls of prickly pear. Teased by spider webs and stung by snapping sticks, we tried to skirt the catclaw, but thorns snagged our Levi's, thorns nicked our socks and shirts and arms, and suddenly a scent of clay dust rose, its fragrance a bit like the smell of blood. We were wearing the river that we'd been waterfighting and mussel-hunting in.

The wash of gypsum salt and red silt was dry on us now, and cracking with each step. Sulphurous, the syrupy smell of crude oil drifted toward us with the river's dust—a slough pit nearby. We'd almost walked in it. We'd gotten distracted watching a scissortail warting a hawk high above us. A primitive music was riding the wind: a pumpjack's squeak and sputter-pop, its long bobbing brass tongue dipping into the cored-out earth, and though the river was behind us, the river was with us: a deep stain of dust that covered our clothes and skin.

## J. PAUL HOLCOMB

# *Blinded by Love*

Signs in Australia say, "This Way Out," pointing to the nearest exit. In the U.S. similar signs seem ambiguous. They say, "Exit," and you don't know what you are receiving. "Stop" is a command. "Exit" is intended as helpful direction. Authorities understand the dilemma. They say the sign's shape details intent, and if you don't obey an octagon you are looking for trouble.

John found himself in a Mexican village, wasn't sure how he got there. After Sarah left him his meanderings had fuzzed in his brain. He studied the town's main street, discovered its tallest building, figured it tall enough. He let himself in, went to the roof and jumped, headfirst. Some minutes later he regained consciousness, realized he wasn't dead. He looked around, convinced himself the chosen building was the tallest. He reentered the front door, went to the roof, and jumped again, headfirst. When he awoke he found himself in a Texas hospital.

Once he was home he began to paint. Desert landscapes and tall adobe structures dominated his work…and sunsets. Muted gold, fading orange described leaving the way he wanted, caused by a distant, octagonal sun.

But he didn't obey the octagon. He would stay each evening on his porch, observe the sunset. When the rays blinded him and he could no longer paint he asked to be taken to where he could sit in front of an ancient Mayan ruin and beg for coins from passing tourists. He asked his best friend to paint a sign,

*"Yo quiero* Sarah," to hang around his neck. But the friend gave him a Susan B. Anthony dollar, asked him to caress the octagon with his fingers, understand its message. His friend convinced him not to go, persuaded him to stop obsessing.

# *Road Hog Two*

**F**ive o'clock on a Saturday morning. "This is a collect call from a correctional facility...."

"Stupid kid! Not again! I'll rip his head off his shoulders this time," I screamed as I kicked the trashcan across the room. Towing costs, court costs. At least he had enough money from his tips to pay his arrest fee. I'd soon be an expert on impound facilities in Harris, Galveston, and Brazoria counties.

Hands shaking, I dialed the Orange Grove Police Department.

"That impound's on Seed Street off Highway Thirty-five," she informed me, cracking her gum every three syllables.

I pulled on jeans and a clean shirt. Grabbing my keys, I tore off to Maizie Mack's house.

"Hey, you awake?" I pounded on her screen door sending racket over the trailer park.

"What the heck you want at this ungodly hour?" Squinting, my fellow waitress opened the door with one hand and lit a cigarette with the other.

"My kid got another DUI," I muttered, fighting tears. "I have to get his truck out of impound and pick him up from jail, so he can get to work by eight this morning." I wiped my nose on my sleeve.

"Sugar, you come on in. That boy will grow out of this phase. Hit the auto button and the java will be ready in a jiffy. I'll get dressed. You can't believe what time I got in. That was one handsome trucker I went dancing with. He's got a real cute friend I want you to meet."

I could do without her account of her latest boyfriend and I certainly didn't need one myself. One ruined marriage was enough and I refused to have any relationships complicating my life.

The coffee aroma enlivened me and after helping myself, I collapsed in the one good chair. What would I do? Rick needed the truck to get to work. He had to work because I didn't make enough to pay his tuition.

Fingers of sunlight tugged at the Houston mists as we set out in Maizie's vintage Chevy truck.

After an hour's search, we found the newest residence of my ex-husband's old Ford pickup. The rust-splotched truck rested under an oak, its injured fender curled like a claw. A huge hound sprawled in the shade, with tongue dripping and sides heaving. Rabbit-chasing. A curious mixture of coffee, motor oil, and gasoline odors hailed me.

Assorted vehicles dotted the impound yard. Two overgrown wreckers proclaiming in flaming letters, "Road Hog One" and "Road Hog Three" hedged the area.

As Maizie lurched into park, I scrambled for the insurance papers and my wallet. The dust had barely settled when a man with "Astros" on his headgear approached us.

"Oooh, check him out, Sugar. See how he...."

"Shut up," I hissed, glaring daggers at her.

"Ma'am, can I help you?" He peered from under a baseball cap which had seen many hours of working under a car.

"Yes, I'm Millie McKay and I'm here for that red truck over there. It belongs to my son."

"Yes Ma'am. Come into our office and we'll get the paperwork done."

I waved goodbye and mouthed my thanks to Maizie before following him to the travel trailer converted into an office. Soft strains of "My Achy Breaky Heart" wafted across the still neighborhood, contrasting with the two slobbering dogs staring balefully behind the wire fence.

103

Did anyone around here ever get in a hurry? At last, the young man coughed politely, his muscles rippling gently under his navy tee.

"Just hand this to the man driving "Road Hog Two" in the driveway now." Smiling he handed me a receipt. "He has your keys."

Rage engulfed me as I realized that I had to go through another person before I could get the truck. That meant additional time, which I didn't have.

Realizing I was going to have to take charge if I expected to leave anytime soon, I marched toward the looming vehicle. Refusing to look at the driver, I thrust the paper over my head and looked pointedly at the ground as I stood tapping my foot.

Finally, the door opened and two long jeans-clad legs, which ended in scuffed Tony Lamas, hit the ground. I looked up and found myself gazing at the widest shoulders and the bluest eyes I had ever seen. I smoothed my hair and wondered if I had any lipstick on. I figured it wouldn't hurt the kid to cool his heels and worry a few minutes in jail.

# *Buzz Saw*

Buzz lay quietly waiting for them to come for him. Such patience was not his style. He'd earned his nickname Buzzsaw honestly: get the ball no matter what, let the chips fall where they may. Today, he'd become one of those chips. Carefully, moving no other muscle, he shifted his focus to where the offending ball lay as still as he did. Nobody needed it now. Just by catching it he had prevented the home run that would have lost the game, shutting them out of the Series.

What a glorious feeling to have leapt higher against the outfield wall than even he thought he could and snatch that ball before it reached the waiting grasp of fans. What a roar of admiration was triggered by its simple plop into his soaring glove. He could have kept rising to the stadium roof, maybe even sailing over to drop the ball right on home plate. Gravity had other plans.

How abruptly euphoria flashed into agony when something—the top of the outfield wall?—conspired to prevent his return to earth with his prize by attempting to rip his arm out of his shoulder. The cheering that filled his ears was instantly blotted out by pain that screamed from his shoulder and blared from every pore of his body. Pain filled all his senses. Absolute, complete, cataclysmic pain.

Then he hit the ground. Neither his legs nor his other arm, stunned by that awful onslaught, did anything to help. Uselessly, his enslaved body crumpled into a heap atop the screaming shoulder.

After an eon or three in the depths of true hell, Buzz noticed that his eyes were open. He came to understand the difference between the darkness and the light, the darkness being the outfield wall and the light a blazing blue sky. A corner of his mind observed, *at least we're not facing the sun.* The jumble along the edge of the darkness resolved into a string of faces all looking at him, wide-eyed. No arm waving, no sign of cheering. Then what was the terrible din that filled his ears?

Buzz thought about smiling at the faces. But he didn't. He thought about finding his fingers and trying to move one, but he didn't. He decided it might be a good idea to get that bright sky out of his field of vision. He sure couldn't afford to sneeze just now. He deliberately blinked. Okay, no harm done. He ran—no, walked—his eyes from face to face along the top of the wall. So far so good.

He risked dropping his eyes to the base of the outfield wall, close enough he could have touched it if he had an arm. He wondered where his left arm was and if—*no let's not go there just yet.* He contemplated the texture of the fresh cut grass. He looked at the ball, so innocent, so still. He wished he could look back toward the dugout. What was taking them so long to get to him?

Some big league athlete! All he could move were his eyes. He confined his snort of self-derision to purely mental. No point in celebrating his one pain-free mobility by doubling the deafening pain everywhere else. This thought tried to bring a sigh with it which Buzz barely managed to fend off.

"Buzz! Buzz boy, are you all right?" A dark blob reeled into his sight.

Involuntarily, Buzz turned his head a degree toward the face on the blob. His desperately maintained stillness shattered, letting pain thunder through his body. His mind jumped up and down with killer cleats on the hateful face and waved murderous fists. Silently he raged and screamed. As soon as he could open his eyes again, he glared with all his being at the stupidest question he had ever heard.

Furball, his pitcher, recoiled from the glare and took that for a no.

Other faces bobbled around him. A fact he had assiduously avoided came and sat on his upturned shoulder, to slobber obscenely in his ear. *You thought you knew pain before, wait 'til they move you onto their stretcher.* The vulture fact punctuated its taunt by delicately jabbing a talon into his arm.

Buzz's mind wrapped itself around that talon jab. His body manned the outposts to face the final onslaught without hope, only courage. A one-man Alamo, a Masada. The light and the darkness dissolved into formless bobbling. He closed his eyes. He never noticed being moved nor the gentle bounce of the medical go-cart that took him to the ambulance. He only wondered why the thundering pain now sounded like applause and cheering. And why it felt so good to sigh.

# JAMES HUSUM

# *Fate's Axe*

Something was coming.

Dan Parkinson knew it on a subconscious level. It wasn't a hunch, more like a deep-rooted instinct. But somehow he knew that trouble lay ahead.

Headlights temporarily blinded him as a car passed going in the opposite direction. Dan sensed it out there. A ripple was running through the fabric of the universe, slowly spreading outward. It would catch up to him eventually. But for now he would keep going about his business

This knowledge was increasing his stress level, making him unsure of everything now. He was working harder but not moving up in the company, putting in extra hours trying to stay at his current level. Money was getting tighter, forcing him to make longer sales trips like this one. His friends and family were becoming more distant. He was losing control of his life.

*There's nothing wrong with your life, Dan,* an inner voice told him. *That's just anxiety. Everyone has that.* This wasn't anxiety though. He had only vague notions of something malevolent, unclear impressions of a force bearing down on him, always pursuing, yet totally impersonal. A deep sense of dread pervaded his every waking moment. It was a matter of time before Fate's axe fell upon him.

A sense of urgency compelled Dan to keep driving, to not stop for food, bathroom breaks, or rest. He had to keep moving, nose to the grindstone, work harder, do more. Keep moving, don't stop, never look back. It was the one thing left that he could believe in. Movement was Life. When he stopped moving, it was all over.

Dan felt ill and found it more difficult to breathe. He needed to rest and his body rebelled at being pushed so hard. *A short break won't hurt,* said the inner voice. His strength was draining away and the need for sleep weighed heavily on him. Dan slowed the car and pulled off on the shoulder. Nausea overwhelmed him, and he broke out in a cold sweat. He closed his eyes and faded into unconsciousness.

Out there, just beyond the headlights, he couldn't quite make it out, but there it was. There was no where else to run, no place to hide.

Something was coming.

# Cowlick

He used to come over for coffee and cheesecake. They would sit on barstools in her cozy kitchenette wallpapered in daisies. She loved his voice, low and thoughtful. Unlike most of the self-absorbed clods she knew, he was sensitive to her moods. He even listened to her opinions.

She liked his intense blue eyes, his hard pecs. His hair bothered her, though. She tried not to think about it, reasoned that it didn't matter. He was ideal otherwise. Why should a cowlick be so important? She would fix her eyes on his face with its fine, strong jaw, willing herself not to glance up at that dorky sprig of black hair splaying up like a peacock tail from the crown.

Sometimes he'd suggest taking her out, but she'd always say, "Not this time. I'm a homebody."

One night he insisted. "I like to try new restaurants, but it's no fun eating alone." So she relented.

He took her to a continental restaurant with red flocked wallpaper and linen tablecloths. She could feel the other diners watching, wondering how she could allow herself to be seen with a doofus who looked like Alfalfa.

She ordered something quick to prepare, hoping he would do the same so that they could eat and leave. But when her food came, she could hardly swallow, for thinking of the stares of those nearby.

He sounded genuinely concerned. "What's the matter? Isn't your chicken any good?"

She made herself meet his gaze and forced a smile. "It's fine. I had a big lunch."

Look at that poor woman, she imagined people saying. What does she see in that bumpkin with hair standing at attention? Can't he get it styled? They felt sorry for her, sorrier than even she felt, perhaps.

Again she reminded him she was the homey type, and to her great relief, he called for the check. She ignored his obvious disappointment, rose quickly and preceded him by several paces to the exit.

Outside in the cover of night, she could breathe easier, and she linked arms with him and chatted, like they did at home.

When he suggested trying another restaurant the next night, she declined. Spending time alone with him was much more enjoyable, she said, and she didn't like him wasting money to entertain her. She thought her cheeks would crack from smiling.

After that he stopped coming, stopped calling. An emptiness plagued her days. She had weeks to think, months of missing him.

She concluded that she would accept him as he was. After all, she had drawbacks, too. Her teeth weren't very straight, and her ankles were getting thick. She would even go back to the restaurant with him if he wanted. The next time he called, she would suggest it, in fact.

After one year's wait, she decided that, in view of their long friendship, it wouldn't be improper to phone and invite him over. She would be nonchalant about not hearing in so long. But her fingers trembled as she dialed his number.

When he answered, she wanted to tell him how much she had missed him, how special he was, how different from the sports nuts and money mongers she had dated since.

Instead she said, "I haven't heard from you in a while."

"No," was all he said.

She gripped the receiver tightly. "If you'd like to come over, I have some fresh cheesecake."

He told her he'd let her know. But the way he said it, she knew he wouldn't call. Beads of perspiration sprang to her upper lip. She knew why he was rejecting her, knew she was the cause of it. She had to get it out into the open.

"It's because of the restaurant, isn't it?" She swallowed and plunged on. "And your hair?"

There was a long silence before he answered. "So you did notice."

She wanted to cry out, Am I blind? Of course I noticed. But she said, "It doesn't matter a bit to me. I'm not that shallow."

His sigh sounded almost like a sob, so she rushed on. "In fact, I've been wanting to go back to that restaurant again."

They made a date for the following night.

When she opened the door to him, she gasped with pleasure. The tuft of crabgrass had disappeared.

Without thinking, she said, "Your hair!"

He reddened, feeling the top of his head. "Is it that noticeable? I've got to get over being so sensitive about losing it."

As he entered the apartment, she saw for the first time the thinning spot at the crown where the cowlick had been. She pressed her lips firmly.

She could never be interested in a bald man.

RONALD W. JAEGER

# Touched by Turquoise

If you were to see Sarah and me walking through Austin's Zilker Park or standing in line at the Paramount Theatre or splitting a "Death by Chocolate" dessert at Katz's, you would likely say what everyone says about us: What does she see in him? This question has tormented so many casual observers I feel it is my public duty to answer it forthwith. You must understand, though, that I am tendering my explanation with some trepidation, for it could be construed as braggadocio.

The first thing you will notice about Sarah is her stunning beauty. You cannot not look at her. She's resigned to all the stares, so she says. But she never resigned to suitors, who, one after another, plied her with gifts to curry her favor.

"One jerk bought me a monstrous chandelier for my apartment," she exclaimed over dinner, our second together. By and by, Sarah discerned that outings with me always fit into a sane budget. I wasn't out to impress her, and that impressed her.

I first met Sarah at a Cinco de Mayo street festival. Tents offering wares lined both sides of the street. In the walkway sluiced a thick blend of skin colors from four different cultures. Strolling the fringe of the press, I noticed a woman in profile holding a wooden mask from which had sprouted multicolored feathers. A wisp of whimsy fleeted across her face as if she was contemplating a purchase for the purpose of spicing up her kitchen or perhaps her bathroom. She put the mask down and turned toward me to roam elsewhere. In that instant I saw it, a medallion of cerulean turquoise suspended on a leather lanyard around her neck. She caught my glance. I winced; it appeared I was looking at

113

her breasts. She eased my embarrassment with a smile that drowned out gospel music floating from a nearby green.

A conversation opened between us as if it were a component of the cosmic order. We migrated over a bridge, down a flight of stone stairs, and along a quiet waterway. We chatted into the sunset, and beyond, and all the way to her car. Before I sauntered off in contemplation of her character purling with peaceableness, Sarah penned on her business card her home phone number.

"Call me," she said as she handed me the card.

"How tough is the competition?"

"There is none."

"Why?"

"You are the first to see the necklace first," she said.

ANGÉLIQUE JAMAIL

# The Fifth Grade Teacher

In her class she likes to play the telephone game

*where you have to pay attention and the lesson is to listen to the message you're being given—I told the children that the laughing cows say moo but they didn't understand why everyone has to whisper and sometimes you can't hear things all that well; it occurred to me when the game was going that maybe there is no real quiet—real silence is only a myth for a nervous mind.*

She's taught for so many years she can't even pretend to think anymore because every time the noise around her stops for a moment

*I want to check to make sure the children are all still breathing because they're never quiet like this*

and she looks around to find herself

*I didn't realize I was alone—where have the children gone to now?*

but she hushes the things around her—the bed, the lamp, the sofa—for comfort until she finds

*I don't matter so much but the children...*

her own life flakes off a little more each fall and

*I become a new person filled with only memories from past school years and soon those all start to run together*

because she doesn't have her own thoughts anymore she exists through the children, a brittle shell protecting her memories, and the children evolve but shells don't. And soon

*I cannot connect even to them now and so I just sit*

I just sit by the window watching the cow laughing on the moon.

GRETCHEN LONG JAMESON

## Stone People Lodge

**B**lue sage breath. Voices of spirit and healer speak. Lavender sparks scent black light. Prayer ties above blessed black, white, red, yellow. They gather to unite. Tunkashila above, and Grandmother Earth below protect those that pray. My skin is white, or is it? Yours is…what color? Does it matter? Memories of land until men, and history gave color meaning…even still…create boundaries. Destroy what is true inside each of us the same. When we stand on the only earth that is whole, not *our* earth, so should the colors mix and ignite…create beauty, if we let them. Fear and faith felt in the dark steamy air. Strength in striving to learn…there is hope. Black thunders, white cloud streams vision, red sacred earth sustains, yellow warmth heals. Knowledge of past events atomic, nuclear…now, cellular. Dark and light in power uncovered. Intellect surpasses ability. When will we learn to leave power simply unto itself, and bow to how it should be? Genetic mutation unchecked we destroy Earth that has given so much. We kill ourselves in power sought for power's sake. Our daughters and sons will die. For what? There is comfort in knowledge they will be safe at last in the arms of spirit. There are those that pray in huts, lodges, churches, temples…to Jesus, God, Allah, Buddha, Tunkashila. The Creators all the same yet, we do not come together as one. Quiet…listen…there is the voice…inside. We have waited and prayed in the womb of the lodge. The Stone People, the Spirits of the Earth speak the ancient language of truth, of compassion…revealed. Black sight.

RAMONA JOHN

# Moving to Dallas

Her hands, blue-veined and fragile now, lie silent in her lap. Her daughters chirp away about how much she'll like not having this big house to keep, and how, with Daddy gone, she'll be far better off where someone keeps an eye on her, and other ladies, now alone, will share her days. One hand flutters up to push away well-meaning words. "But what will become of my cat? And who will tend my azaleas then?" A quick squeeze of her shoulder, "Now, Mom, it'll be okay." "This is my home," she says, "I came to Smithville as a bride. Here is where we raised you kids. It's where your daddy died." They start packing, discarding, sorting through drawers and chests, pictures and clothes, the treasures of a lifetime. Silent now, she strokes her cat, cradles it close. She tries to picture how her house will look, how it will feel, alone and empty after fifty years. And deep within her heart, she knows. The vacancy has begun.

# *Goodbye, Harry*

**W**hen Harry choked on a prune and died, his widow Marjorie was sorry, but not devastated. They had always lived on her money, had few common interests and Harry had never been a particularly loving husband. Still, she was fond of him, and she'd respect his wishes.

He had often mentioned his horror of being buried in a box and how he detested the pomp and fuss accompanying funerals. So she'd have him cremated, skip any service, and scatter his ashes at the seashore.

She called the crematorium, and they told her it would be a couple of days before they could take care of Harry. They'd had an unexpected rush.

The following morning, Marjorie's doorbell began ringing wildly. A woman with tousled hair and lots of jangly jewelry stood outside.

When Marjorie opened the door, the woman shouted, "If he wasn't dead, I'd kill him!"

"Kill who?"

"Our husband."

Marjorie stared at her. "You'd better come in."

"I'm Jasmine," the woman said, "When Harry was out in Las Vegas two years ago, he swept me off my feet and married me. I should have known something was fishy. Always off on those sales trips."

Marjorie said, "You're sure you're talking about Harry? My Harry?"

Pulling his picture from her purse, and waving it before Marjorie, Jasmine said, "Our Harry." She sniffled. "To think I loved him."

"How did you learn about me?" Marjorie asked

"A friend who was visiting here happened to spot him being wheeled into the hospital," Jasmine said. "I took the redeye into town, but he was already dead. They said his wife had claimed his body. I'm glad he choked. Serves him right."

Then she began wailing. "What will my friends say? I'm so embarrassed. I can't believe he's put me in this spot."

Silence. Then Marjorie said, "There's no reason anyone has to know."

She stepped to the mantle, where Harry kept his mother's ashes in an urn. She handed it to Jasmine.

"I've already had him cremated. Take his ashes. I know he'd want you to have them. Just hop the next flight back to Las Vegas and when you can, scatter him in the ocean, like he always wanted."

With thanks and more tears, Jasmine left.

Marjorie called the crematorium. "I've changed my mind."

She phoned the minister of the largest church in town, and arranged for Harry's service in the immense sanctuary. She promised a very large donation to the building fund if each detail of the funeral was exactly as she requested. Then she invited everyone with whom Harry ever had even a nodding acquaintance.

Harry's sister, Agnes, arrived from Baltimore and was bewildered. "But Marjorie, Harry was an atheist. And I thought he wanted to be cremated, like Mother?"

"Strangest thing," Marjorie said, "He had a vision of his mother, just the day before he died. It led to a religious conversion. Changed his mind about everything."

Agnes said. "Speaking of Mother, I'd like to take her ashes home with me, now that Harry's gone."

"Oh, didn't he tell you? The cat knocked her urn off the mantle and broke it. We vacuumed up what we could and sprinkled her out back beneath the jasmine. That was Harry's favorite flower, you know."

Marjorie had him dressed in the old purple bathrobe she had been trying for months to persuade him to throw away.

"But surely his pin stripe suit might be better?" Agnes suggested, "He was always so proud of his appearance."

"Nope," Marjorie said, "I want him to be comfortable throughout the ages to come. And I want to remember him the way I saw him most often."

Those who attended the service spoke of it for months. Boom! Boom! Boom! went the drum. The bugle sounded, and solemn men in tuxedoes rolled in Harry's open casket, followed by the choir, singing "Onward, Christian Soldiers."

Harry lay in an ornate coffin with cherubs covering its lid. Those who came forward to view the body were furnished rose petals, and invited to scatter them over Harry and his purple bathrobe.

The light from a blinking neon cross cast a bluish glow on Harry's face, as a young woman in a frilly dress read selected poems by Edgar A. Guest. The organ played softly, and the scent of many floral arrangements hung heavy in the air.

The minister, who had never met him, praised Harry for an hour, inspired by Marjorie's generosity.

As twelve somber deacons carried Harry to his eternal rest among saintly souls buried in the churchyard, the choir sang "The Hallelujah Chorus."

Marjorie waved a lacy handkerchief and called, "Goodbye, Harry!" She smiled bravely and said to Agnes, "It's such a comfort to know I gave him exactly the send-off he deserved."

# CHARLOTTE JONES

## *My Feet*

My feet have changed. They used to fit beautifully into an 8A. Now they have grown longer, wider. Suddenly I find myself asking the clerk for a 9B. Toes spread so that only square-toed shoes are acceptable to them. Callused heels opposite thick and jagged nails catch on the sheets at night. No longer are my feet willing to accept the accoutrements of the well-dressed leg. Toes cry out when suffocated in panty hose and seek their revenge by proffering a corn or two. Balls and arches shriek in dismay when faced with high-heels. I have moved south so that I might go barefoot most of the year.

Each day, I stand on these feet and gaze into the mirror, pluck a few grey hairs, watch my neck grow crepy, and wait in dread for my ears to grow long and floppy and my parents to die.

# CHARLOTTE JONES

## Safari Nights

I am exhausted yet uneasy. It is my first night in Kenya. We sit around the campfire under the clear twinkling sky, drink whiskey, and savor the roasted leg of impala. Other than the chattering of a few monkeys, the acacia forest is still. Finally, as the embers burn low, we stumble to our tent and fall into our bunks.

The night is moonless and there are no city lights within a thousand miles. The darkness wraps around you like wet velvet.

"Do you think we'll see a lion tomorrow? Maybe an elephant?" I ask my husband.

"I'm sure we'll see them all, honey," he answers, his voice already a sleepy mumble.

He just begins to snore when I hear *whoooOP! whoooOP!*

"What's that?" I jump, sending the covers to the floor.

"Some kinda critter!" He is wide-awake now.

*No kidding.*

ARF!

"That a dog?"

"No dogs out here," he declares.

*We've been in the African bush for twelve hours and he's an expert already.*

*EEEEERCHaaaah! EEEEERCHaaaah!*

"My God, sounds like someone stretching on a rack! Tribal rituals, you think?" Our imaginations run wild. How can anyone sleep?

*OOOOocah! OOOOooah! HO HO HO!*

"What the hell is that?" His whisper is urgent.

"Maybe a lion." I shudder as I wonder which of those ten immunizations I got will protect me from a lion. I get my covers back on the bed and dive under.

"That's not what a lion sounds like, not like that lion at the beginning of all those movies, anyway."

"Everyone knows that movie lion roar is not how a real lion roars. It's faked with computers or something."

"Well, whatever it is, it's too close to the tent!" He fumbles for the propane lantern, but can't find the matches.

"Shhhh, I think I hear it breathing." I exhale as my own breath adopts its pattern, *ee-haaa, ee-haaa, ee-haaa* in-out, in-out, in-out.

It is quiet for a few minutes. Too quiet. I hold my breath.

*Scitter-scitter-scitter-scitter.*

"That's right outside our tent," he hisses through clenched teeth as the tiny feet flitter across the canvas. "In fact it sounds like it's IN our tent."

SNAP! A twig breaks somewhere near the front of the tent. A grating, rubbing sound begins and the entire tent shakes; the supports creak in rhythm.

I grip the covers to my neck, hold my breath, and listen wide-eyed to the Kenyan cacophony. I wonder if I should tell him that I didn't pull the tent zipper all the way down.

CELE S. KEEPER

## *cinema verité*

black and white images flicker across the screen as larger than life movie monsters with scaly reptile skins, eyes blazing, belching fire, salivating from mouths of jagged teeth stalk unwary prey and tear them limb from limb, while we watch, shuddering, screaming, transfixed in horror, a metropolis succumbs to panic, concrete streets crack open, buildings topple, molten steel girders fold in on themselves, women shriek, children wail, families huddle in fear and all will fall victim to this rampaging beast

then, to quell such unspeakable evil, the hero arrives in a pith helmet, disrobing in a phone booth, on a shiny black steed, in a charging Batmobile, racing to the rescue, demanding justice, sworn to defend the defenseless, to put things right once again

now we live in a different world: our monsters arrive in innocent airliners, in letters where virulent spores lurk, in a growing hatred toward us which we somehow neglect to acknowledge, but prayerfully, not in our water supply, nor as the flesh-eating Ebola virus, nor in the deadly guise of cyber-terror

this time, how can we be sure the good guys will win?

CELE S. KEEPER

# *Mistaken Identity*

**W**ailing sirens and flashing lights playing patterns on our wall woke my brother and me in the middle of the night. We nearly knocked each other over scrambling to the window.

Squad cars and THREE ambulances were at the corner house where the weird Vansickles lived. Neighbors in their pajamas were spilling outside.

Pop roared in, "Boys, come away from that window. RIGHT NOW. This is none of your concern." He left before Lou and I could ask questions.

Which, of course, left Lou and me with our imaginations working overtime. All of us kids on the block thought these people were really strange and snooty. They'd been there two years and not one of us had been inside their house. Our moms had asked Mrs. Vansickle over for coffee and she turned them down flat. Mom said she wasn't even nice about it.

We'd see their kids, Audrey and Alec, who were about our ages, riding off in their private school bus. They never even said "Hi." Tearing by on our bikes, every now and then we'd see their father backing out of the driveway. The place was like a tomb: doors, windows, drapes, shades all shut tight.

So, we did what kids do: We sat in our backyards on sticky, summer evenings, swatting mosquitoes, scarfing down homemade cookies and lemonade, and made up stuff about each member of the Vansickle family.

Tommy, the oldest and kind of our leader, went first. "Mr. Vansickle is, for sure, a member of the mob, maybe even a killer. That's why he's gone so much and never wears anything but black."

Lou was itching to go next. In a scary voice, he said, "I bet Mrs. Vansickle has a horrible skin disease with drippy sores all over her face. That's why she hides in her house." Davey really got into it then, "I'm sure she's a witch. My guess is she makes goofy noises and cooks up smelly potions to cure herself, but nothing works. Doesn't it scare you guys to think she could put the whammy on any one of us?"

Mookie, wide-eyed and our youngest, swallowed a cookie in one gulp. In a shaky voice, we could barely hear, he said, "And I bet that old lady is teaching Audrey to be a junior witch. What if she turns us into horny-toads, or lizards or even worse, icky ole bats." We all shivered at once. Then I added my two cents, "To me, Alec looks like a natural born killer. He's really spooky, just like his old man." About that time, our parents called us in.

Lou and I headed back to the window, as soon as Pop left. No way would we be surprised at ANYTHING that happened to those creeps. Watching as four stretchers were rolled out, we really freaked out. The sheets were all the way over the tops of their heads. This wasn't play-like anymore. Those were DEAD bodies and neither of us had ever seen one.

Shivering and silent, we slunk back to bed. When Lou asked if he could get in with me, boy, was I glad.

Our Mom tried to hide the headline in the morning paper, but we were too fast for her. There it was: HIT-MAN MISTAKENLY EXECUTES FAMILY OF FOUR. Mr. Vansickle was not a mob member. His company made toy stuffed animals for little kids. Lou and I nearly wet our pants when we got it that the killer had goofed and murdered the wrong people. The guy who did it told the police he'd made a mistake.

When Mom put breakfast in front of us, Lou and I, for the first time in our lives, couldn't eat a bite.

JULIE C. KEMPER

# Oak Trees

**A** pair of them, a wedding gift to the first owner of our home, stretch across our lawn, witness to many lives. They held sneakered feet of robust curious boys, a swing for cradling baby or sweetheart, and a set of chimes that still sound in the wind like the pure tones of a Gregorian chant.

These live oaks define my day from first view through dimpled shutters when I scan their rough elephant-hide bark for playful ripples of sunlight chasing curve and niche along an elegant labyrinth of limbs.

One day, I watched a flood of iridescent grackles swarm to these twin towers with raucous cries. Above, I discerned, in the nimbus of the tree, songbirds who kept their simple grace until ambushed by this explosion of sleek, long-tailed birds when they fled their perch from twisted limbs. One by one their sweet songs grew silent as they disappeared into a brilliant sky.

## MARILYN GILBERT KOMECHAK

# *Target Practice (Christmas Eve in West Texas)*

The shooters from across the border fire at their own empty beer bottles but stop when the sheriff pulls up. He says he's only lookin' to do a little target practice, still they crawl back into their trucks to drain a few more cold ones. Spanish music blasts to mix with handgun and rifle shots echoing off the mountains bathed by a cold sun's slanting rays. The sheriff sits down on the ground and leans back against a post to unholster a silver six-shooter mounted with a large scope.

From behind the safety of their windshields, the men watch us, a small knot of Anglos standing under a corrugated tin canopy, while the sheriff gives instructions. "More than likely all missed shots are due to lack of trigger work." Then with a Colt Magnum bullet cradled in his palm he shows us how it dwarfs our 22 long. "This one can do more killin'."

Before I can assimilate his words, it is my turn. In the scope of a deer rifle I find the concentric red circles. There is the eerie silence of men watching. I take careful aim and squeeze the trigger. As we walk out to the target, the ground littered with shards and tattered paper, our boot soles crunch brown glass.

I remember how the sheriff watched his back when he strolled to the target. I fight the urge to look over my shoulder. Then, bending down with our heads together, we see it: Bull's Eye. A voice rises clear carrying back to the men under the canopy and in the trucks: *Good shootin' Mom.*

129

# WILLIAM LAUFER

# *Pratas Reef*

South China Sea, and running hard against filthy monsoonal weather, Manila to Hong Kong, when the starboard lookout reports he smells fresh-tilled earth and says it is land birds he hears calling from the starboard hand. Adamant in fear's face he is.

Minutes later we are hard aground on coral heads, our twin screws turning idly, slightly awash in the surf. Four hours and nine minutes into the beginning of a new day. The Morning Watch: foul weather and cold, with gulls cursing our intrusion into their space.

This is Pratas Reef, 160 miles southeast of Hong Kong. The climate is reliably thick and hazy in the vicinity of the reef, and soundings give no warning of close approach to it. Current and tidal rips prevail in the vicinity, and are frequently mistaken for breakers. It is an unmarked, unclaimed pile of coral and detritus remaining from the mercantile efforts of incautious and unfortunate shipmasters. The salvage crew requires eight months to refloat us and make whole our holed bottom, using tons of ping-pong balls and Styrofoam for the task.

The true essence of reality is dread mingled with angst: fear hangs behind all things as does the specter of hope. We live in the thin space between two doors—hope and dread.

That first night aground Mr. Mayhill, the navigator, dreams of his appearance before the long green table. I, on the other hand, dream of High Tea, Guinness Stout at the Peninsula Hotel in Kowloon, and the charms of Madam Wu who waits behind the first door in that palace in the East.

## Questions Come at Night

Often in the deep of night something tugs you from the dream's door, and they begin again, circling in your mind like the last record on the turntable, repeating and repeating all the old questions, questions that rise, shrill as a flute's cry, to fall away unanswered.

Through the black tent of night stars flash their cosmic code from unthinkable distance, a code that may never be broken. A west wind leaps the mountains and whispers secrets to the pine forest. It speaks a tongue long forgotten.

Often in the night you can hear it—how the universe hums with meaning, how at times you can almost hear the words. Sometimes a door begins to open, a slow wedge of light starts to fail. Then as you reach, crying, "Wait!" you find the door already closed. It stands, solid as stone, dark and indifferent, while questions, like frantic fists, go on beating and beating....

MARY ELAINE LORA

# *Her Civic Duty*

The air was heavy, hot; and everything in Jackson Square wilted under its weight. Everything except Miss Veronica. A white silk gardenia bloomed on her navy straw hat. A collar of white linen with a crocheted edging rested crisp against her neck, the only adornment on a shirtwaist dress of navy rayon. One white-gloved hand held an open umbrella to shield Miss Veronica from the afternoon sun; the other held a small Gus Mayer bag.

She walked first around the perimeter of the square, surveying the artists' work. Many of them greeted her by name. Artists, she thought, belong here. It wouldn't be Jackson Square without them. They add...color.

She entered the square then and walked deliberately toward several benches in the shade. She chose a vacant bench, closed her umbrella, and smoothed her dress as she sat. Removing her gloves, she saw but willfully ignored the faint orange splotches on her parchment-like skin. She put the gloves in her purse.

There are fewer people today, she thought. The heat has done that. Without realizing it, she smiled. They are all hiding inside with their air conditioners. Ah, but the birds, the birds are always here.

She placed the bag on her lap, reached in and drew out a handful of bread crumbs that she tossed to the pigeons. "Come, my darlings," she cooed. "Come and feast." Eat, drink, and be merry, she thought, but she didn't say it. "Come, little birds. Come see what I've brought you."

The pigeons heeded the call, flying down from the statue of Andrew Jackson, trotting over from under the bushes, bumping into one another in their eagerness.

"Oh, how greedy you are, little ones," she said and laughed.

Suddenly another creature approached Miss Veronica's bench. She smelled it before she saw it. A man or what might have once been a man. Now it was just a mass of greasy, matted hair and beard topping a body shrunk too small for its ragged clothes. It slouched onto the bench, and Miss Veronica inched toward the opposite end.

"Feeding the birds, huh, lady?"

"Yes." She looked at him with eyes as blue as a glacier. For an instant the tiny lines in the creases seemed to grow longer, the faint tracks across her brow turned into furrows.

"Lot of people don't like pigeons. Say they filthy. Crap all over General Jackson there. But me, I like 'em."

"Yes, I thought you would," Miss Veronica said, still tossing out the crumbs. "Kindred spirits."

"Ain't as many pigeons here as there used to be, though."

"No," Miss Veronica said, smiling.

"Not near as many."

"No." The smile spread across her face.

He sat up and reached for her hand, which she instinctively withdrew. "Say, where you get bread like that? Ain't never seen that before."

"I make it." Pride crept into her voice. "I buy fresh whole wheat bread every day, cut the slices into one half inch cubes, sprinkle them, and toast them in the oven for precisely seven minutes."

"Sprinkle them?"

"Yes."

Her bag was empty now. She folded it and put it in her purse. Then she put on her gloves, rose, brushed the front of her dress, and opened her umbrella.

"Well, good day," she said looking down at the man.

"Huh? Yeah, sure."

134

Miss Veronica strode out the square. What a filthy little man, she thought. And the nerve to sit by me with the stench of cheap wine all over him. She turned up Chartres Street and walked briskly toward home. She wanted to tidy up. But the thought wouldn't leave her. What a filthy little man. She stopped suddenly and giggled in delight. Tomorrow I'll bring him a sandwich.

# Toward The Source

Ominous are the clouds, green the pine trees to each side of the road over which the tires are flowing. Silent is the space called atmosphere. Vacant is the road before us. Endlessly, we roll on over the cushion of moisture mile after mile after mile. "This" moment comes and goes and this sameness continues. No planes are seen in the sky. No birds are winging. Weather warnings are out for all, and yet here we are endlessly moving toward the source of the ominous clouds. Like life is this; we continually move from one day to the other cushioned by our faith. We endlessly move to our death, with ominous clouds of frustration and sorrow, until our destiny overtakes us, always moving onward, forward toward the source and its complete conclusion.

# ANNE MCCRADY

## *Building C, Apartment 12*

They turned off the electricity today, just as she was slipping her finger down the knife-edge of the second overdue notice. In the darkness that descended like ashdust, she felt the blood seep into a crease along her knuckle. Stumbling to find a Bandaid, she kicked over the trashcan, spilling empty chicken pot pie boxes and soda cans across the peeling linoleum. The noise was deafening in the echoing dark. Desperate for light, she pulled loose the skin of black plastic the last tenant had tacked over the windows for illicit privacy and daytime sleep. The damp winter grayness of January flooded the kitchen. She sucked it in like a grateful first breath after a long swim to the surface. Shaken, she thought about her freezer-full of groceries, the recent gift of a churchwoman who said she could remember her own hungry days. With the electricity off, the ice cream would begin melting. Already a seasoned if exhausted survivor, she tried not to panic as she assessed her situation: no lights, no stove, no microwave, no refrigerator, no television, no hot water. Squeezing her cut finger against the heavy throb of blood trying to escape the pressure of the bandage, her eyes blurred. The apartment became a watercolor wash of angry abandon and putty-brown walls. Looking up, she saw her distorted reflection in the dull mirror of the oven door: twenty-two, single, pregnant and now no utilities. The avalanche of people who could say I told you so, threatened to smother her. Hot desperation swelled in her throat. She wanted to run or to hide or at least to make a phone call to a friend and cry....

as if she had a phone...or a friend.

BRIGID K. MCVAUGH

# Farmers' Market

City Hall presides over the Rose Garden, sunlit white, trimmed in green. Wooden stalls fence the square as women promenade the perimeter, pushing babies, carrying straw totes to bring home earth's bounty. See the green-garbed Silver Queens, Super Sweets and Sugar and Cream, picked fresh, plucked up, picnic fare for the suburbs. Cucumbers shine without wax, and need not shed their jackets for salads. Beets and carrots, pulled from the garden's brown blanket by their green ponytails, bunch in baskets. Plump purple eggplants, once lavender blossoms, lie in voluptuous repose. Broccoli bought here needs a brief soak to evict pale green tenants from its branches. Zucchini, yellow crookneck, and pattypan give way to hard-shelled spaghetti squash and butternuts as the weeks turn toward October. Bell peppers become more red than green. Bees and children hover along Church Street, competing for a taste of cider or a slice of an early Paula Red apple. The early bird gets a basket of black raspberries.

Sheaves of glads spill jewels down Main Street. A woman with long brown hair hauls her cutting garden in buckets in the back of a Ford Explorer. Large or small, she asks, square and graceful hands poised to paint a still life. Meadow posies mix with garden blooms as she composes a bouquet. From her palette she chooses a plume of purple loosestrife, blue bachelor buttons, black-eyed Susans, and a tall-stalked white lily. Deftly she wraps the bunch and bestows it like a gift.

Tonight I will set my table with this feast, food for the body and flowers for the soul.

138

# LIANNE ELIZABETH MERCER

## *Connection*

You're a kid, and you lie on the scratchy August grass with your chin in your sweaty hand watching ants gathering crumbs, and you ask where they're going, and they don't say, just crawl over blades, between blades, beneath blades, and you stick out your finger, and one steps on and stops, and you look close with one eye, and you see three brown lumps, six legs, antenna waving, and then the ant curls like melting butter onto your arm, and you feel the happy tickling of its steps clear to your soul, and you watch it drip off your elbow into the grass and disappear into the heart of the earth, and you wonder how it knows when to move on.

You're not a kid any more, and you walk with him on October days spilling over with sky, blue above you, beside you, between you, and you anoint your body with sun gleaming on red maple leaves until your skin burns with joy, and you are hungry for the heat of the man who lies against you in the night, the happy melting together and the curling toes, and you ask him if he's staying, and he doesn't say, but his hand feels like moonlight sticking to your fingers, and you awaken in your cold November bed alone beneath satin sheets the color of goodbye, and you unwrap another kiss even though you know your life won't ever taste the same.

BETH MILES

## In Need of a Lifeboat

Her razor-sharp tongue slices through heart and mind and nerve like a ship's keel cleaving an ocean of memory in its wake. His barbed response severs the bond of companionship like his fish knife skimming the scales off a life that's done. Age and infirmity render them unmindful of all they used to share, unable to recall sunlight embracing the crest of a wave. And we, their children, grieve and swear we'll never be like them. Then, sailing on a sea of adversity, our regard for each other slips overboard on skids of caustic words and disappears beneath the breakers. And our children grieve and swear they'll never be like us.

# Lost in North Houston

Traffic is bumper-to-tailpipe and we're barely moving. My eyes are drawn to the driver of the BMW in front of me. It's easy to see the woman is vein-popping angry, but I'm pretty sure it has nothing to do with gridlock. She jerks her head toward the passenger beside her, jaw snapping in staccato time.

Occasionally one scarlet-tipped stiletto finger slashes the air in his direction. He just gazes out the side window, his profile a less-turbulent semblance of hers. I decide he must be her son.

His refusal to acknowledge her attack seems to add fuel to her rage. Her demeanor becomes even more agitated, her body language a chronicle of malevolence. I think I've never witnessed this kind of hostility directed at another. I wonder how the boy can remain so passive. Surely words delivered with such fury must inflict pain.

My breath catches when his door swings open. In one fluid movement he is out of the car and running down a long alley. The woman erupts from the driver's door, screaming at him, but he is gone, vanished into the shadows that lay along the walls. She stands for a moment beside her vehicle, glaring into the dimness.

I peer into the gloom also. I want to think he's there somewhere, waiting for her to come and bring him back, to end the harangue.

The metallic snake of waiting vehicles is edgy, coiled to strike, horns blaring in dissonance. There's been movement up ahead, and the woman's car is now the one blocking the way.

She shrugs her shoulders and raises an arm to deliver a one-finger salute to her fellow travelers. With a last glance down the darkened alley, she slides in behind the sleek leather-covered wheel and drives on.

I gape in disbelief that she would just leave the boy that way. The restless horns urge me now.

"Hurry up, Mom." My youngest son speaks from the seat next to me, anxiety shading his voice. I hesitate and squint again into the murk between the buildings. But there's nothing to see.

I look at the brown-eyed adolescent beside me with a tug of gratitude, and my spirit weeps for another brown-eyed boy lost in the streets of Houston not so long ago. I wonder when Mrs. BMW will know this was her son's last ride.

# HALLIE MOORE

## *Ablution*

**W**hispered threats tunnel women's bodies pulse with thick breathing uncles one of us snatched dragged by the hair over broken glass our cries ignored in the genes a permanent panic. Now this hollow public restroom alone washing up amid acrid tile rust-stained sinks and toilet bowls exhale a chalky "Hey you, come here!" a lipless no tongue sound daring me to scream my ears strain listen for the screwy pale-eyed guy who slouches off movie screens into women's bathrooms into that fulcrum moment run for your life or trust one more time. Reckless I peer under no boots shuffle no pants drop squint up no red tongue waggles through the vent nerves electric I yell "Hey, yourself!" slap stall doors open their swing and pop exposing not one pervert hunched on the fixtures this Thursday morning. I slam flush every toilet wrench the taps on race from the purging.

## RITA NESBITT

# It's All in the Point of View

*The Bat:* It was early spring and I had been late getting home. There I was, my wings wrapped snugly around me, hanging from a root on the flimsy ceiling of our cave. I had only been asleep a couple of hours when I felt the roof tremble. My wife grumbled sleepily that Bear's hibernation must be over.

Suddenly the roof opened. A screaming human tumbled in and together we plummeted to the floor, landing with a bone jarring thud on top of Bear. Before Bear or I could take a breath a second human landed with a crash and a shout on top of us.

Bear rose up on hind legs, his face a mask of confusion and surprise. He gave a bellow of panic and charged from the cave. And I charged with him; my roost was entangled in his fur and for a moment I was too stunned to let go. As we crashed through the forest I could hear my wife's squeaking complaints about the dust and debris fading in the distance.

"I will never, ever, again," I vowed as I returned to my equally indignant wife, "share a cave with a bear!"

*The Bear:* It was early spring. I knew it was spring because a vague feeling of hunger was beginning to stir in my slowly awakening brain. I heard the Bats mumbling and I wished they'd hush and let a poor bear sleep.

Suddenly there was an ear splitting scream and something hit my back and knocked the wind out of me. I tried to sit up and catch my breath when wham, something landed on my head and knocked me cross-eyed. Sticks and leaves and dust were thick in the air and I could smell humans.

"Good heavens," I roared, "I'm under attack! It must be hunting season." I bolted for the door and freedom. As I

144

crashed through the forest I could hear something squeaking angrily in my ear. It was Bat! He was tangled in my fur.

I vowed I would never, ever, again share a cave with a couple of bats. They were, well, batty.

*The Heroine:* It was early spring. It was that time of year when a man (young or old) turns his fancy to romance. I had let Mr. Judd talk me into going fishing at his stock pond, and he had brought along a lunch—Church's fried chicken and the whole nine yards. He'd been chasing after me all winter, and I knew what he was after. He intended to get a little sugar in payment for the fried chicken.

As I dashed through the woods in pretended flight with Mr. Judd in playful pursuit, I suddenly felt the earth beneath my feet open up and swallow me. I landed with a thud on something soft and furry and warm. And then Mr. Judd was crashing down on top of me.

Something big and black reared over us, let out a terrible bellow and disappeared. I was too stunned and surprised to be frightened, but I wasn't going to let him know that.

Mr. Judd caught his breath and laughed, put his arms around me and said, "Now, now, little lady, don't be scared. I'm here to protect you."

Of course I snuggled up close and said, "Oooooh," as though that was all I could say.

Mr. Judd looked smug and masterful and said, "Now, about that fried chicken, I've chased you long enough."

As his lips pressed mine I gloated, "Yeah, and I caught you." But I did wonder why that squeaking noise I heard reminded me of my mother's nagging voice warning me about a certain type of gentleman. Ah, well, I'd think about that another time, maybe after the fried chicken.

145

REECE NEWTON

# ℜew Territory

**D**arrell and I played army often. I wanted to be a cartographer, so I would convince him to help pace off where we were playing so that I could map it on graph paper, planning our operations. Darrell wasn't as interested in the finer points of war but liked to charge around with a full backpack. He always had some money to spend on gear for our adventures, and in those days, there was plenty of interesting stuff left over from World War II at the G. I. Surplus store, where we sometimes went on Saturday mornings. I didn't have as much money but made up for it by making the maps and by setting up field communications, stringing wires for some old working telephone handsets that I had scrounged. Darrell had a big machete with a canvas scabbard and an aluminum canteen with an olive drab canvas cover that always gave a slug of water a funky scent like the inside of a musty tent. There were binoculars, tin cups, and other interesting devices that had been too cheap to pass up. Thus laden down, we set out on expeditions that our eleven-year-old imaginations drew from Columbus, Lewis and Clark, and John Wayne.

We were supposed to stay within the boundaries of our flat backyards, but the woods beyond beckoned with steep drop offs, narrow ravines, trees for climbing, and thickets for cover. My folks trusted me not to go down there; Darrell's had threatened him with a whipping if he went. They said there were snakes, or we could fall and break a leg, or the occasional small-game hunter might shoot us. Of course, that made it irresistible, so whenever we figured we would not get caught, off we sneaked.

One fall day we loaded up our gear, skirted the thick bushes at the edge of Darrell's backyard, and slipped down into the woods. Checking over his shoulder, he said, "Mother would beat the tar out of me if she knew I was down here, and with my B-B gun!" Darrell's parents knew but didn't mind that he had such toys as the machete, and they had bought him the gun to use strictly in his backyard for practice, shooting a target pasted onto a cardboard box stuffed tight with newspapers. He had gotten pretty good at it.

Five minutes into the woods, we scrambled down a ravine to where a trickle of water ran. Sitting on logs, we ate our peanut butter and jelly sandwiches, washed down with tent-tasting water from the canteen. I got out my clipboard, pencil and paper, saying, "This terrain is so rough, we're going to have to do some hard climbing to map it."

Just then we heard a chatter and looked up to see a squirrel on a limb halfway up a nearby tree. I put the binoculars up to my eyes, adjusting the focus to get a better look, when a sharp pop right by my ear startled me! Dropping the glasses, I saw that Darrell was pointing the B-B gun towards the squirrel's tree. Then I saw the squirrel, quivering, trying to hold onto the limb, finally falling with a soft rustle into the leaves below.

We walked over to the tree. The squirrel wasn't dead, but lay quivering, its eye half shot out. "What did you do that for?" I hollered at Darrell. I somehow felt as if I were up in the air looking down on Darrell, me and the squirrel. Mechanically I noted that it had been a pretty good shot.

"Now, what am I gonna do!" Darrell's voice quavered. "I was only supposed to do target practice in the backyard! I'm gonna get it now!"

I stood there frozen, then said, "What did you want to shoot that squirrel for, anyway? You didn't need it for food. And now you can't leave it like that." But the army guy shouldered his gun and started scrambling back up the slope, crying a little. I looked back at the squirrel. My mouth tasted metallic, mixed with the peanut butter and the tent water. In the equipment that Darrell left behind was the machete. I used it, but it was as if someone else were using it. It clanged on a rock, gouging the blade in a way that we could never grind out. My throat felt as if a balloon had been blown up inside of it, hard, and my stomach felt perhaps like Columbus's men had felt when they were sure they were going to sail off the edge of the world.

VIOLETTE NEWTON

# The Hollow Room

They bend under museum lights in their white coats, carefully peeling layer from meshed layer of broken, brittle cloth to bare this apelike vessel which stares up but does not see. Unravelled distance falls away here in the windswept line of sloping brow, the frozen thrust of jaw.

Round, like elliptical suns, like moons and the earth itself! But who can catalog fire gone out? Can man catch it in a can, fold it in a book, bid it stay? All that was beautiful and bright leaped in those eyes, ran like a mad ravishment in the heart and brain, bursting in glory and pain, flashing, flickering, burning, drifting its cinder, leaving its ash.

Sly machines may separate the laminated years, clicking data on marvelous tapes, but only blood which courses the living vein may measure the emptiness of vein sans blood, only the living eye may see where no eye is. Man alone, breathing the breath of God, can feel the pitch of this tent where the spirit long ago moved on, leaving a hollow room, as all rooms are when God is gone.

# A Woman's Prerogative

He never wanted to but he went ahead and opened the purse. There were compartments. He didn't have a clue what the use of so many sections could be.

He'd heard on a TV show that it was a woman's prerogative to keep her personal life bound up in her purse.

Slowly, like pulling a hot filter out of one of those newer model cars, he managed to remove her wallet from the purse without disturbing too much.

There were the two snaps on the wallet. One. Two. A threefold contraption. He laid the entire thing flat on the table next to his empty coffee mug. He took a deep breath. Mildew. Another scent. *I've got Windsong on my mind.* That brought pain with it.

The first fold of the wallet, a clear plastic window, revealed her face on her Club Membership card. Taken years ago when big glasses were the rage. Made her face look small, petite, so very pretty.

The next fold held her credit card. She had only one stuck in the slit. She believed in that, one credit card. Put everything on it, she told him. Pay one bill at the end of the month. He didn't cotton to that much. Then there were the library cards stuck in the other slots. One library card for each of the kids. Funny. The kids were in college now.

The last fold held a packeted plastic folder. The driver's license. The kids' pictures. A family picture, the last one they had taken. Years old. Her insurance card long expired. The video store card, checking account card, beauty store discount card and membership card to the book club. (He'd been working for months to get that canceled.) He pulled and tugged the last tiny shred of paper sticking out of one obscure slot.

The paper fell like an errant autumn leaf at his feet. He stooped to pick it up. He unfolded the tiny scrap, soft with much handling, and laid it flat on the table next to the wallet.

It had been a year. One whole entire stupid year.

Energy had gone with her passing. Couldn't work. Couldn't go anywhere. Could only sit and watch the news, flipping channels.

He had only recently gotten around to clearing the closet. Had Goodwill in to haul the stuff away from the garage. The only thing left, besides that little piece of purple 'n white paper for income tax purposes, was the purse. And the wallet.

Good memories? He'd been a good husband. Came home every night. Not like some. He'd paid the bills. Bought a big house, five bedrooms for cryin'-out-loud! A king could live in a house like that. Or a queen.

Five bedrooms.

He worked long hours. Worked like the dickens.

Sure she'd complained. Made him mad. He bent over backwards to scrape together what they had. She'd told him she wasn't happy. She wanted more.

"More what?" He demanded to know.

"I don't know." She replied with tears in her eyes, muttering something about living.

Didn't catch her exact words.

"What do you call this?" He asked her. "Dying?"

He smiled at the thought of how he'd won that argument before it had even started.

But he still hadn't found a note.

A reason. Dammit…why?

With the contents of her wallet strewn about on top of the kitchen table with last weeks dishes and stacked pizza boxes, he knew as certain as certain is that she had left him long before she actually had.

151

He stared at the photo that she had hidden in her wallet. The man in the photo stared back at him from atop the table. Didn't know him. Didn't know him from Adam. No movie star. Just a basic looking guy. Basic. Nothing special.

He stared at the photo.

A woman's prerogative.

CLAIRE OTTENSTEIN-ROSS

# The Girl in the Purple Dress

My art instructor was a lady as colorful as the paintings she created. Especially fond of purple, she mixed it into all her paints, blended it into purple-green trees, purple-red flowers and purple-blue seas. We learned how to combine her favorite color into everything our brushes touched.

The day the doctor told her she had cancer she began a brand new painting. A small girl stood alone on a beach gazing out to sea. She wore a purple dress and held three purple balloons that reached upward into darkening clouds.

She said the picture represented her. The child looked to the far horizon for an answer to her illness—for courage to get through the dread disease. Our teacher never finished her painting. She died within months.

Now, when I work on canvas, I can remove the colors from my hands, but no matter how hard I try, I can never get the purple out of my heart.

# LISA L. POWELL

## *Luda*

Rising in an early morning hour, you shepherd your sleepy children to a school where they face daily battles trying to be understood and trying to understand. You then walk wearily to your small cubicle at the small beauty parlor to gamely lure uncertain clients onto your masseuse's table. Kneading and rubbing, you shunt the tightness and stress. Kneading and rubbing, you avoid the endless struggle and the children's persistent questions you can't fully answer. Kneading and rubbing, you transcend into that state of mind where you don't have to think about anything anymore.

Returning in a late evening hour, you shepherd your sleepy children into a bed where they dream fitful dreams of snowball fights and babka. You then quietly crash into your tattered recliner in your tattered apartment to capture a moment's rest before the pushing and pulling of dingy mops across grease-stained linoleum. Kneading and rubbing your bleary eyes, you think of your mother in Yoshkar-Ola. Kneading and rubbing your throbbing temples, you remember you forgot to pay the electric bill. Kneading and rubbing your bent neck, you desperately wish for someone to send you into that state of mind where you don't have to worry about anything anymore.

## LISA L. POWELL

# Official Response

Lauro shut off his computer, leaned back in his chair, and rubbed his temples. It was already 11:00 p.m. He pondered sleeping on the old recliner crammed into a corner of his cluttered office. There was no reason to go home, really. He had sent his wife and young son away earlier in the month when things began to get too hot. The memory of their goodbye drummed in his aching head.

"Why couldn't you have been an architect?" she had murmured, her wet face buried in his neck.

The response had been swift once the officials discovered that he was snooping around and asking the wrong questions. Tinted sedans cruised slowly like sharks past their modest walk-up. Ringing phones in the dead of night revealed only silence when answered. A strange, little hobgoblin of a man began shadowing his every move. Lauro could have avoided this situation entirely if he had minded his own business and kept filing his pedestrian stories about the comings and goings in city hall. The lies and corruption engulfing his city slowly began eroding his indifferent shell. Lauro was on to something big, and he couldn't look away anymore, even if it meant putting himself and his family in danger.

Lauro's eyes rested on his wife's photograph, and he smiled wearily. Maybe he would go home, curl up in her chair, and watch that ridiculous late night telenovela that she, at that very moment, would be watching, too. He reached for the phone.

"Augustin, I'm ready."

Lauro grabbed his jacket and briefcase and waited for the portly night watchman. He hated being so precautionary. It was conceding to them a small victory; he had been intimidated. The two quietly made their way to the street below.

155

"Good night, Augustin," he said, plopping heavily into his car. It suddenly occurred to Lauro that he had missed his regular goodnight call to his son.

"Godspeed sir," said Augustin with a tip of his hat. He turned and walked away, pausing briefly to nod to a peculiar, elfish man standing in a nearby doorway.

Lauro sat for a moment looking at the modest downtown skyline sparkling like a New Jerusalem in front of him.

"Why *couldn't* I've been an architect?" It would be his final thought.

Lauro placed his key into the ignition.

# CARLYN LUKE REDING

## Points Further East

The night traveler navigates Houston's rivers of traffic, enters the easterly flow leaving red ribbons in his wake. Long lines of light diminish at dawn revealing highways and byways with bridges over swamp and bayou, river and creek. Overhead an eastbound plane from Hobby catches the jet stream racing the traveler to points further east. Psyche, the traveler's constant companion, hovers above the melody of a Vivaldi concerto slipping from the silver disk swirling under the dashboard. From her vantage point, she narrates a running commentary of the plane's long view of the Big Thicket, the Natchez Trace, the Blue Ridge Mountains, the Atlantic. Notes county seats, state capitals, churches and universities. For fun, counts counties into states. Then, they visit the birthplace of Liberty, presidents, and generals, weep at the tombs of the famous, the common man and the Unknown Soldier. The traveler checks the compass, the car veers east, he wonders what is east of the point. From her realm of music, Psyche just smiles and keeps the secret.

# Look Up

The heat of summer had been torrid. There had been no rain for over one hundred days. Water was rationed. I had given up watering my backyard, hoping the deep-rooted trees and shrubs would survive. Yet their leaves drooped, the flowers planted from seeds died.

Because of ill health my spirits had drooped, too. Then one day as I started to visit the doctor, I looked at my back fence and was amazed at a sunflower nodding its head above the fence. Its lemon yellow petals contrasted with its jet black center. It was only nine inches wide, not the nursery variety, but there it was in the hot wind, lifting its head to the sun.

My mood changed. It brightened my life for several days and then another bloom came in its place and continued to glow until the rains came. I remembered that no matter how unhappy we are, it pays to look upward.

# Squall Line

The storm comes quickly, without warning. The bright sunny day turns ugly. Wind and rain pound the sea with unexpected force. Fierce waves crash over the bow, then surge in foamy torrents across the foredeck and flood the cockpit. The tiny boat is no match for the eight-foot wave which takes its mast and rigging into the churning, frigid water. Suddenly, the wind dies, the overcast lifts. Last rays of sunset spread across the shimmering water. The boat continues to dance, but this time without a partner.

ALVARO RODRIGUEZ

# The Dogs

**I** call him dog, and he comes to me. He sits on the floor, content. Without words, we nourish each other.

I saw him in a shop window, as the story goes. I had to have him, so I went in with my open wallet. The storekeeper was sad to see him go, but took my money.

I call him dog, and he comes to me. Since the first day I brought him home, he was trained. He does things. Without my telling him, he knows exactly what to do.

I do not let him out at night. I cannot bring myself to let him roam the streets, looking for a heated bitch. It does not seem to bother him: this house, this room, this chair, this floor.

I call him dog, and he comes to me. He has a birthday coming up. I will buy him Milkbones and we will celebrate. I will bake a cake and we will eat it, the frosting on our paws and cold noses.

They will bury him with me. Side by side we will sleep. I call him dog, and he comes to me.

# ALVARO RODRIGUEZ

## *Orion's Belt*

Chris is my father's name. It's really Cristobal, but he passes for White, so it's Chris to everyone who meets him. My mother's name was Elizabeth, and she was White, but I used to call her Elisa and pretend. She never knew about it.

My mother died seven months ago in a car wreck. She was alone.

Our last name is Vela. It means "candle." We pronounce it "VEY-la," even though it should be "VEH-la." A lot of people at school don't know I'm really Mexican. They think I'm Italian, at the very most. I try not to let it bother me, who I am.

When my mother died, I was at Danny's house playing Donkey Kong on his Atari 2600. This was the big home video game before Playstation2 or X-Box, before Super Nintendo and Sega, and way before CD-ROM. Danny thinks it's cooler than playing those new games with great sound and color. He says it's retro. He says he'd play his Pong game from Radio Shack if it still worked, the piece of shit. But his Atari still keeps on ticking, even though the joysticks are pretty messed up.

Danny's mom was the eighth person on a list of parents my Dad called that night. He was crying like a baby. She said yes, that I was in Danny's room, and he told her my mother had died and would she please tell me to come home. That's just the way he said it. I know, because that's just what she said to me: Mitch, your father called. Your mother has died and he wants you to come home.

Danny says his mom's a bitch. He says he wishes she'd have died instead of my mom. I told him it wasn't good to say things like that. He said his mom was a piece of shit.

When I got home, my Uncle Timoteo and Aunt Belinda were there, consoling my father. My grandparents on my father's side were dead, so they weren't there, except maybe in spirit. My mother's family was in Boston. They had forgotten about my mother when she married my father. Even though my father passed for White here, my mother's family never thought so.

I came into the dining room where my father was sitting and he hugged me, hard.

My back hurt from the way he hugged me.

He said everything was going to be all right, that she was in a better place. I didn't cry or look weird or anything, but I did ask him what had happened. He couldn't tell me. He just started heaving with big sobs, and put his head down on the table. His arms were wet with his tears.

My aunt sat me down and told me my mother had lost control of her car on the freeway and had plowed head-on into a tree. She wasn't wearing a seatbelt. She went through the windshield.

Her head was open and full of glass.

Larry came to the funeral. And after that, he was always around. He would cook for us, clean for us, and he was always staying over. My father cried a lot, all the time, and Larry would look over at me and smile but I didn't smile back.

Then it was my birthday and Larry made a cake. I wanted Danny to come, too, but Larry didn't think it was such a good idea with the way my father was feeling. I want to make it up to you, he said. Happy birthday. He gave me a big red box.

I opened it. It was a telescope. So you can see the stars, Larry said. Then he handed me a book. This is from your Dad and me, he said. From both of us. It was a book about the constellations.

That night I woke up. My mouth was dry, my head felt hot. I got up and walked down the hall to my father's room and opened the door.

My father and Larry were sleeping together like Danny and me would when I went to his house for an overnight. Only they weren't wearing pajamas, and Larry was wrapped around my father, their backs to me.

I saw that Larry had a tattoo of a black scorpion on his shoulder blade. It raised its pincers and clicked them, then walked around his back, down his spine, and under the bed sheets.

I went back to my room. I picked up the book Larry had given me and then I pointed the telescope out the window towards Orion. Orion is the Hunter. He has three stars that make up his belt. The center one is called Alnilam. It was blinking, on and off, like it was going to explode.

# JANE BUTKIN ROTH

## *Glimmer*

When I was a child, it visited me. It entered through a strand of light at my bedroom door. Or it arrived on a stray moonbeam that my child-spirit caught effortlessly back then. But I, being a child, was ill-prepared for its coming or its leaving. Still, it was mine—in my house, in my grasp. I know because I felt it when feeling was knowing. But I couldn't make out its words or memorize its formula. I was too small, too innocent to think I should have been paying closer attention. As simple and fleeting as a flicker. Or a caress. A fingertip slightly grazing my sleepy head. Some sound I heard, but couldn't define. A whisper. A whoosh this side of a breeze. A faint chorus in the next room. Some small rustling—of grains or dust, wind or insects—just outside my window, inside my dream. But, it didn't stay. It left quickly. What took it? My own shrill voice that could discourage? My solid footsteps that might trample such a thing? Perhaps it had somewhere else to go.

But I was less prepared for its leaving than its arrival. And I have been preparing ever since. Mostly, I try to notice. And remember. I think that you may be bringing it, that you are my possibility, so I listen carefully, so very carefully. Come back to me…. But the sounds are more scrambled now and I am not so sure as I thought I would be. I've waited so long for it to materialize, to show itself, to replace this remnant memory of leavetaking and lost light. Am I too tired from my own old longing to receive what you might hold for me? Will I miss that beautiful, delicate thing I have been waiting for?

## DONALD WALTER SAMP

# *Caged Spirit*

He sits on a large perch, hunched over, behind huge metal bars, at the zoo. White crested head identifies him from others of his species. Here there is no place for him to fly or soar, so here he stays perched, not to fly.

For a hunter's buckshot brought him down. Frightened and in pain, he crawled to safety and hiding. There, a kind soul found him, took him to a local veterinarian. He was healed, rehabilitated, except he remained wing wounded.

So here he is, in this huge zoo cage meant for lion or tiger, with nowhere to fly, nothing to hunt. An unfamiliar bare place—not home. Stooped over in sadness, longing for the air. Then as if his thoughts were received by nature's ear, a gust of wind rushes between those barrier bars, and the eagle straightens, raises wings as if to fly. One wing is awkwardly bent, the anchoring limb. As the wind continues, to him, he is soaring again.

For a time, he is fishing at spillway waters of his river's dam. Soaring gliding and diving through hazy blue skies.

Then breezes subside and he returns to his former pose. Years pass, nature completes a cycle. The proud Bird of Freedom falls from his perch. But in a far off nest, near a dam's waters, an eaglet is born and the spirit of an old eagle is reborn.

In time, this young eaglet will mature to soar, fish, and hunt again—uncaged.

# NAOMI STROUD SIMMONS

## *Keeping the Water Hot*

What to do when your whole life has gone to war, your spirit boarded a train to Jersey, boarded a troop ship heavy with body ballast for the winter Atlantic crossing, England? France? How do you fill your days? You bake cookies. You bake for the U.S.O. with rationed sugar, fold bandages with the ladies of the church, knit olive drab scarves with a limp fury, write V-Mail, and say his name, pray his name, write his name, hoe the Victory Garden, anything to stiffen the limp marionette you live inside. And in a movie at The Paramount an anxious father, John Wayne, boils water as his wife gives birth. I return home, pray, bake cookies, pray, write letters, pray, and boil water.

# THOMAS SPIRITI

# *Sarah's Detour*

Sarah couldn't believe she was actually having a breakdown. She was crying silently but urgently while standing in the pet department of Wal-Mart, staring blankly at the numerous dog, cat, bird, and fish supplies even though she didn't own a pet.

She wasn't concerned that she was missing a tennis match at her club, an important one that she had arranged. Normally she would never miss a match and would chastise anyone who did. And she wasn't worried that her friends would be angry. She could easily make up a story about the maid or the cook or some other employee that would explain why she was so late—if she decided to go at all. Either way, she would avoid any hard feelings with a clever story, with anything but the truth. Now, though, she needed to be alone, or apparently she needed to be at Wal-Mart.

This odd experience began with the phone call from the women with whom her husband was having an affair. Actually, the affair was over, which is why the other women, the rather optimistically named Sunny, decided to call Sarah and tell her all the sordid details.

Sarah had suspected for several months that Charles was cheating on her. At first she told herself that she was just being jealous, but as evidence mounted, she tried to ignore it by working harder on her backhand, planning lunches, dinners and evenings out with friends. The phone call today simply jarred her into a reality that she had tried to avoid.

Afterward, she came to Wal-Mart where she once shopped for everything she and her mother owned. Meeting Charles had changed all of that and, in fact, had changed her life entirely. She knew that if she married this older, wealthy man she would never have to worry about money again. She also knew that one day he would cheat on her. This was instinct likely gained from her hardscrabble life and the men her mother dated. Nevertheless, Charles was her chance for a new life, and Sarah took it in spite of her doubts.

Glancing around quickly and taking a deep breath, she began to feel in control again and wondered if she had come to Wal-Mart to escape from the only world she knew now to the one she had known before. She had married Charles just days after her mother's death and, until today, had lost all contact with the life she and her mother had shared.

Real tears began to flow.

"Are you all right, baby?" said a voice that startled Sarah into awareness of the ridiculous way she was acting.

She turned and peered into the face of a very large black woman. It was a face of pure kindness and concern with an expression that Sarah had not seen in a decade. Suddenly, she felt the crashing need to cry out, to sob, to let go, but she knew she couldn't because the tenderness she saw in the woman's eyes was so powerful that she could lose herself in it.

"I am fine," Sarah said with force and, it seemed, anger. "Please mind your own business and leave me alone. "

Shocked at her own words, she realized this stranger, even more than Charles, her friends, her employees and herself, knew that Sarah was not fine, that she was hurting, alone and frightened. Sarah could never bare her soul to this woman, although God she wanted to. The stranger's expression did not change, and Sarah's desire to tell her everything was almost overpowering, but she forced herself to turn and walk away.

I am fine, now, Sarah thought and holding her head up, she walked out of Wal-Mart.

As the top of her Lexus lowered, she began to formulate the story she would tell her friends at the club. She actually smiled for the first time that day as she planned her exasperated recital of the latest maid mishap, knowing that was something her friends would not mind listening to and would understand.

CATHY STERN

# Court Street Notes: Brooklyn

Walking here in winter, plucked up by plane from humid Houston, put down in a matter of hours into this grey almost foreign world, I feel the space I'm used to disappear. Its absence presses in, building upon looming building, shop after small shop, a proliferation of banks, pizzerias, greengrocers, offices, bodegas, schools, laundries, doubled and redoubled as if by the sorcerer's apprentice. I pass by more people in twenty minutes than I ever see in a week at home—so many faces, a bobbing assortment from everywhere yet most with the same turned-in gaze, a multitude fragmenting toward a thousand destinations. Odd languages swirl and rush past me, clearer bits of conversation float by: a British accent tells a child, "It's *not* alright if she spits at you at school!" A tall woman, two very long dachshunds on a double leash, murmurs, "Come along, piglets." And now, in front of me, a short, stout person, sex undeterminable, wearing many pairs of socks and assorted layers of clothing, pushes the familiar grocery cart overflowing with bulging plastic bags, contents unseeable, a huge, pink paper flower rising from one side like a flag.

SANDI STROMBERG

# *Ascension*

*A video/sound installation by Bill Viola (2000)*
*Museum of Fine Arts-Houston*

I descend the *calanques* outside Cassis. Follow their chalk white cliffs deep into the sea. And lulled by the echoes of oxygen meeting water, I leave a trail of bubbles to the Mediterranean floor, my death mirrored in the black face of the deep.

The corridor curves like a capital "S" from the bright white of the museum into a darkness black as the womb, black screen on black wall. I stare into nothingness. Listen to the ricochet of low, eerie sounds. Then, a heart-shattering explosion quakes the room as a body holding a Christ-on-the-cross pose plunges into the water. The sea effervesces. Bubbles form the halo of a numinous double. The body ascends and I think *Ascension*. But no, it only releases air. Then descends...descends... descends. Alone. Sinking below the surface of the screen. Only the water breathes, accepting the sacrifice. Seconds tick like hours. Then, bubbles transubstantiate. Luminesce. Rise.

Fear shackles me. Though I poise to break the placid surface of a no-longer-serving life, black dreams come. I freeze, afraid to release bubbles of breath. The past. Afraid to descend. Alone. Afraid to fall off the screen of my present life. To make the sacrifice. To allow the water to relinquish my spirit. Until I, too, can experience ascension.

171

ELLYN TORNES

# No Place for a City Cat

**I'm** knee-deep in wild raspberry vines and striped with scratches, searching for a missing cat.

"Circe!"

Something brown scurries off, the wrong color. Circe is black with white front paws that look like she started to climb into a gallon of ivory paint.

A tractor hums in the distance where Toby Moss is baling hay.

"Hey, Toby!"

Peering through a haze of exhaust, he gives me a curt salute. My mother's nearest neighbor, Toby was never quite right after a jeep accident took his right leg and cut short his military career.

People here have a propensity for losing appendages. My father, missing two toes, said it was an occupational hazard of farming, but a sharp knife or garden tool was as likely a culprit. My mother lost a fingertip while cooking for a wedding.

I trudge back to the farmhouse where my family has lived for five generations, though it's just my mother now. I left for San Francisco ten years ago, a shabby suitcase in one hand and a college scholarship in the other, with nothing severed but family ties. She has never forgiven me for leaving.

"Did you find it, Jane?" My mother sits on the back porch with a big plastic bowl between her legs, shelling peas.

"No. Guess Circe wanted a little adventure." My attempt at conversation plops like a dead mouse at her feet.

"Silly to bring a house cat here on vacation." She pushes a strand of drab brown hair from her face, reminding

172

me of something scurrying in the vines.

I pick at a scratch on my arm. "I didn't know what to do with Circe."

"What kind of name is that?" She stops shelling and peers at me like she did when I told her I wanted to be an English teacher.

I start to answer, but other words struggle for voice. I want to tell her about the Bay, the classes I teach, odysseys, the novel I'm writing, the man who left me.

"Circe was a witch who turned men into swine."

"A witch." She sets the bowl on the table, shaking her head. "What kind of heebie jeebie stuff did you learn in California?"

Around suppertime, Toby lurches up the porch steps, reeking of hay and exhaust fumes.

"Something smells good," he says, wiping his neck with a kerchief.

*It certainly isn't you,* I almost say aloud. "How you doing, Toby?"

"Five bales done."

"Sit there, Toby." My mother points to a chair next to mine. I hope she has given up her dream of seeing us wed and uniting the farms. My chair knocks Toby's prosthetic leg with a dull thud, but he doesn't seem to notice.

"What were you yelling about outside?" he asks.

"Circe, my cat, ran off."

My mother offers him more noodles.

"What does Sir Sea look like?" Toby asks.

"She's black with white front paws." I don't explain my cat's name. No telling what Toby would make of witches and swine.

"She?" Toby looks puzzled. "Sir Sea's a funny name for a girl cat."

"Let the man eat his supper," my mother says before

I can answer. I poke at my food until Toby pushes his plate away and burps.

My mother's eyes light up like high beams in a fog. "Cherry pie?"

"Later," Toby says, patting his big belly. He turns to me. "Maybe I seen your cat."

"Where?"

"Come on, I'll show you." Toby gets up and sticks a toothpick in his mouth. Outside he lumbers toward the field in a lazy zigzag.

"Cir-ceee," I call.

Finally he stops and points to a surreal patch of black and white in a hay bale.

"No!"

Toby chews on the toothpick. "It's only a cat."

"She's my pet!"

Toby shrugs and I pound his chest in fury. Losing his balance, he tumbles backward like a toy soldier.

I run to the house. My mother sits on the porch, holding something in her broad lap.

"What's all the commotion?" she says. From the folds of her faded yellow apron, Circe purrs.

"You found her!"

"It came back by itself, full of fleas and briars."

"Circe, I thought you were dead."

"Don't be so dramatic." My mother frowns, handing Circe to me. "Where's Toby?"

Crimson faced, Toby limps up to the porch. "Ain't no place for a city cat," he mutters.

"I thought she was in the hay bale."

"Guess it was just a coon."

My mother stands up, brushing off her apron. "Ready for pie?" The screen door slams behind them. I sit on the steps, stroking Circe and picking briars from her fur, feeling more tattered and less at home in this bucolic setting than my errant California cat.

174

# STEPHEN VILLARI

## The Real World

The night sky passed away as the sun began to creep over the horizon. A cool mist still hovered over the grasslands making it crisp to the smell. The tall blades of grass danced back and forth at the whim of the wind. Everything was right with the world.

He opened his eyes slowly and eventually rose to all fours. For two days now he had been asleep, but even then he felt drowsy. After a moment of sleepy contemplation he began moving towards the faint light.

Light flooded the small creature's eyes and he shut them. Soon everything became clear and shapes of wonder filled his head. The sun was now above the horizon and the world had suddenly come to life. Birds of song flew overhead, squirrels went about their endless harvest, and young mice scurried over the soft ground.

The creature pranced down the incline; his armor clanked against his belly. He made his way over the meadow and finally to a small creek. He looked up and down the banks to make sure it was safe and finally stuck his snout into the cool water.

A shadow cast itself over the creature and all went silent on the meadow. The squirrels and mice ran for cover and the birds of song returned to their nests. However, all was calm in the mind of the creature with his head still under the water. Suddenly, a sharp pain filled the animal's mind and he screamed. The sharp pain continued until finally a sense of happiness and peace returned to the body.

The hawk stood up and looked down at it's kill. It was happy at what it had accomplished and let out a proud squawk. It filled its beak with meat and flew back to its young. Everything was right once again.

175

## BEV VINCENT

# *The Sad, Short Life of a Blue Ceramic Bowl*

Perry searched the crowded silent-auction room for the item his former lover had contributed. Whatever it was, no matter how high he had to bid, he meant to have it. It would be a bittersweet memento of a brief, exciting time of ill-advised passion that had almost destroyed him.

He found the handmade blue ceramic bowl nestled between an autographed photo of a local celebrity and a set of champagne flutes. The bidding sheet listed her name as the donor. Perry increased the opening bid by fifty dollars.

For the rest of the evening, he hovered nervously, watching to see if anyone bid against him. As the deadline approached, a flurry of participants vying for the most desirable items blocked his view. Perry edged nearer, transfixed by the awkward blue bowl, beautiful only to its maker and to someone who had loved her.

His shoulders relaxed and his heart rate returned to near normal when the auctioneer ended bidding. Perry pushed through the crowd to claim his prize, quickly paid and departed.

On the drive home, he contemplated the bowl. He valued it not for its craft—for it had none—but for its maker, who had kneaded the clay with her delicate hands, shaping it with fingers that had once traced the lines of his face. Her creation immortalized a piece of her heart, capturing it beneath a fire-hardened glaze. Her fingerprints were preserved in the abstract whorls decorating the bowl's sides; her initials were permanently etched in its base.

Her very aura emanated from this artifact. Liz would come to understand how important it was to him, how much he needed to possess it.

Even so, he left it in the car when he got home that evening. It rode beside him to and from work while he considered how to broach the subject with his wife.

Their new routine included a nightly walk around the block. Sometimes they strolled in silence. Other times they spoke only of inconsequential events from their daily lives. Occasionally they discussed how they felt about what had happened.

Close to the halfway point, a streetlight illuminated an otherwise secluded portion of the path. Here, even in the midst of an emotional discussion, they always stopped and kissed.

"I've got something to tell you," he said as they rounded the first corner.

Concern creased her face. He winced at the insecurity he read in her eyes. That was his fault.

"I bought something last night," he said. "A bowl."

She remained silent, looking straight ahead as they continued down the sidewalk.

"She made it." Since the reconciliation, neither of them had spoken her name. It hadn't been a conscious decision, just another way of coping.

She released his hand and stepped away, turning to look at him, astonishment etched in her face. After several seconds, her trembling lips formed a single word. "Why?"

"You're upset."

"Why would you want to commemorate the most difficult time in our marriage?"

"I can't explain," he said.

"I never want to see it," she said. "I don't want it in our house."

They continued to the halfway point in silence. Liz almost didn't stop but relented when Perry took her hand and drew her close.

"Okay. I'm sorry," he said after they kissed.

He put the bowl in the trunk of his car. It stayed there for several days while he considered what to do with it. He contemplated giving it to one of her friends, or putting it in his office as a candy dish.

Liz never mentioned it.

Four days later, he invited Liz out for lunch. "A picnic at the park," he suggested. They ate deli sandwiches on a bench beside the lake, watching parades of ducks weave through the water. When they finished eating, Perry took his wife's hand and kissed her.

"I love you," he said. "Only you."

Tears welled up in Liz's eyes.

"Wait here," he said. He returned from the car carrying a brown shopping bag. Liz regarded him quizzically.

When he removed the blue ceramic bowl from the sack Liz gasped. In the midday sun, Perry realized for the first time how ugly the bowl really was. The work of an ambitious amateur.

Without a word, Perry gripped the heavy dish and threw it as hard as he could. They watched it sail through the air. An enormous geyser erupted when it struck the lake's surface. For a horrifying second, Perry thought the bowl wasn't going to sink.

Then it was gone, plummeting to the bottom of the murky water.

Perry turned to his wife. Tears streamed down her face. He took her in his arms and held her, staring over her shoulder at ripples that grew and dissipated when they reached the shore.

SUE PETERS VOLK

# Interrupted Dreams

Emma woke with a start. Had she heard a noise? She was wide-awake, shivering in the cold. The wind was howling outside, and the room was light as when there was a full moon. But it was the wrong time of month for that. It must be snow, dancing in the wind outside the house. She thought the children in the town would be excited to wake up to a white world.

Now that Sam was gone, dead over a month, she should be glad to hear the conversation of the wind. She listened. Silence, except for the storm. Probably another nightmare; she'd had many since Sam's death. As she relaxed she pondered her life, almost over, and how quickly it had flowed. The good years and the bad, all muddled together like marbled icing on a cake. Her childhood, parents, siblings, and girlhood friends. College. Sixty years of marriage to Sam, a golden thread of comfort and security that had held her together, given her strength through the ordeals with their son Paul. Now, thirty years later it still hurt, like the phantom pain of a lost limb.

Well, life was still worth it, she reflected. More goods than bads in the long run.

She'd better just get up, make a cup of tea and read another chapter in her novel. Sleep would elude her, maybe until dawn. She turned on the bedside lamp and stuck her feet into the sheepskin slippers, pulling her maroon flannel robe around her shivering body. She took her book off the bedside table and padded down the stairs.

Emma heated the teakettle and retrieved a mug from the sideboard. Her fingers sorted through the assorted teabags and found chamomile. She lit the gas fireplace in the kitchen and was glad for its instant cheeriness, regretting that she'd

179

argued with Sam about converting the wood-burning one. She loved it now. Soon the kettle whistled and she prepared the tea and began to read.

*Thump.* This time it was real. A chill ran across her shoulder blades. The sound came from the direction of the front porch. She turned off the light and stole through the dark hall to the bay window in the living room, the lace curtains brushing against her fingers as she drew them aside to peer out.

There was something there, huddled on the porch against the front door. A dark indistinct form. A large dog? A human, taking refuge from the storm? The porch, with bay windows on either side, formed a protection from the wind in this small mountain town.

What to do? Certainly not open the door. But on this frigid night someone could freeze to death. She shuffled back into the kitchen in the back and turned on the light. She looked at the old mantle clock. Three-twenty.

Something had to be done. She picked up the phone and dialed nine-one-one. She gave her message briefly, stated her address and hung up.

Ten minutes later, from the bay window she saw headlights approaching, red lights circling on top. The EMS van fishtailed as it fought its way up the snow-covered hill. In front, two men jumped out and began running toward the house. Suddenly, one stopped and shot his hand across the front of the other. They approached cautiously and bent down on their knees and gently pulled. A figure uncurled. She heard murmurs, and then an urgent voice saying, "Can you get up?" followed by an indistinct man's voice. They helped a man struggle to his feet.

*He's alive. Thank God I called in time.*

The doorbell rang. She turned on the porch light and opened the door, shrinking back from the icy blast.

The vagrant stood slumped, graying head hanging,

180

an arm slung around the shoulder of each man.

"Ma'am, don't worry, we got him. You okay?

She nodded. "Is he all right?"

"Can't tell yet. We'll call you after we've examined him. He'd a' frozen for sure, though."

They struggled down the steps with their burden. As the smaller man sprang to open the van door, the vagrant's head turned and with distinctive bottle-green eyes, looked back at her.

"Wait!"

The EMT turned questioningly.

Emma's knees buckled and she knelt in the doorway, hands clenched in fists over her mouth and tears blurring the snowy night.

"That's my son."

LORETTA WALKER

*Awakening*

Morning sunlight pierced through trees and songs sung by seven dove could be heard in background. Gentleness of early morning has made an entrance. Orion's belt has long disappeared, and happy endings of fairytales lay shut on the nightstand. Scent of sandalwood still covers half burnt wax and steam of hot tea has dissipated with night visions I do not remember. Sleep removed my awareness of transition of night to dawn. Nonetheless, I am satisfied with morning sunlight piercing through trees.

GERALD WHEELER

## *The Garret Builder*

The garret builder led me to his project in his backyard—a kid's dream tree house overlooking Lake Travis and a green forest.

But my gaze and camera were drawn to an image a few yards away. An image that I'd not seen since I visited my grandparents' farm a half century ago.

Like grandpa's bib overalls, long johns and bandannas drooping on a cable wire between live oaks, the garret builder's jeans and socks told the story of the man who created poetry with his hands.

Patches of colors—cobalt, swirling storm clouds, black as midnight, and a creamy twilight horizon, each held precariously by two wooden fingers across nature's garden.

Only jeans were topsy turvy, like a boy dangling on a branch upside down. One pair had knee stains of the clay beneath.

A tattered, bulging clothespin bag decorated with daises, was tethered to the middle of the line like an heirloom separating family belongings.

And an empty wicker basket, its straw arms reaching out like a child wanting to be lifted, stood patiently under the swollen bag.

No wind.

Only a portrait of people akin to sky and earth, who live among wild grass, cacti, live oak and pine. Paradise bordered by a leaning, rusty fence, "to deter deer and stray cows."

The only sounds—a saw humming, cracks of the garret builder's hammer, rustling leaves, and a soft woman's voice offering the visitor a glass of well water.

GERALD WHEELER

# The Sandcastle Builder

The sprawled child with tiny feet that looked like milk-colored footpads slid deeper into the sand. Her pale arms and hands moved as rhythmically and relentlessly as the waves, digging and filling a green plastic bucket with sand, turning out pail-shaped bricks she wedged into place on a multi-tiered sandcastle with the dexterity of a mason. She worked diligently, alternating her gaze through opened flip-lense sunglasses between the wet sand reflecting like celluloid film in the hot morning sun and her growing creation.

A few feet away, bare arms across her chest, a statuesque woman stood in ankle-deep sand. She stared out to sea through dark-tinted glasses like a ship's captain searching for danger. Like the child, she wore a yellow T-shirt, faded jeans, and had the same light-brown hair escaping in a long ponytail out the back of a red ball cap.

A safe distance away near the moat protecting the sandcastle, a row of sandpipers balanced their fat chestnut and white plumaged bodies on a single wire-thin green leg, their black curved bills uniformly slanted toward hidden crustaceans like frozen jackhammers.

Suddenly, a pair of flying nymphs with shoulder-length golden hair, wearing neon-orange bikinis, leaped into the air and executed a series of cartwheels, forward hand-stands, and back flip-flops. Finished with a roundoff salute—landing together, feet planted in the sand, arms extended to sky, back arched, head proudly tilted backwards, their posture accentuating their massive manes. Then, reversing course, their sinewy legs flexing in measured strides, the nymphs raced past the front of the sandcastle, furiously kicking up water and sand, destroying part of its defensive walls. They ended their display in a trio of somersaults, a handstand, wildly running and diving into the surf.

The half-buried child in a yellow T-shirt and red cap executed damage-control—madly hoeing piles of sand toward her. She paid no heed to the attacking waves, frolicking nymphs or to scurrying sandpipers. As she baled and scooped water and sand, her torso was sinking faster and faster. Water was flooding the ramparts, gushing up to her armpits. Her face was almost touching the foaming water. But she refused to retreat. Incredulously, the tall woman standing vigilance did not budge. For a moment, all one could see was the top of a red cap and light-brown ponytail floating on the surface of quicksand. Until her immersed arms and shoulders miraculously appeared and her delicate fingers gracefully moved like a Siamese dancer. Until she slowly raised her contorted body like a gymnast on a pommel horse, liberating her withered, powerless legs. Then, using only her elbows and palms, she maneuvered her sand-coated body, making short, deliberate crab-like movements in the sand, dragging her dead legs and footpads behind her as she retrieved scattered tools and started dredging a moat, fashioning bricks and ramparts. As before, under the shadow of the woman now eyeing the flapping simulated hawk wings of a bird kite flying over the pier.

Ten minutes later the guardian retreated to their base for a wheelchair with knobby tires. She pushed the iron chair toward the builder making final touches to her castle. The tall lady motioned to the sitting child to reach out to be lifted. But the child glanced upward, continuing molding bricks. After an eternity coaxing, the caretaker knelt in front of the sand-castle builder, slid her hands under the child's arms, raised her to her chest like a papoose with dangling puppet limbs and carried her to the wheelchair.

She lowered the wet child on the towel-covered seat, wiped her little girl's rose-colored face with the bottom of a dry T-shirt and waited. Waited patiently for the rider to buckle the seat belt. This achieved, the tall woman moved beside the wheelchair.

The sandcastle builder tightened her lips, placed an iron grip on the hand-rims beside the knobby tires, her ponytail swaying in the breeze. She pitched her small torso forward in the high-back chair, vigorously working her strong, small disciplined hands along the chair's hand-rims, wheeled ahead, beginning her journey in waves of sand splashing Galveston's 2.5 mile seawall—the longest mural in the world—an endless painted relief of undersea creatures, seabirds, and colorful native symbols, all swimming in a turquoise sea created by the hands of 14,000 child artists. She started at the humpback whale.

CYNTHIA K. WIER

# *Vacancy*

The house is numb with quiet, scattered with books, ghosts of voices left behind.

They are gone for a few short months, but their leaving has quelled the clatter of phones ringing, baseball games blasting from the TV, and the dull blare of music behind two doors.

Now there's the loud stillness of one empty room after another. I follow relentlessly my list of tasks: car wash, picking up tickets for a concert, calling for the cat's annual check-up, and then in and out of the grocery for tonight's dinner, one they wouldn't like.

It will take some time to befriend this new silence, to replace the sounds of boys growing up. I'll set two places with blue crystal, thin white china, and we will begin.

# BETTY WIESEPAPE

## *My Father in Sepia*

My father, a young man in this photograph, is standing beside his best friend, his best friend's girlfriend, and a young woman with largish legs who is not my mother. The four of them are standing in a line beside steps that lead up to a white house with round columns and a wide porch.

A Model A Ford sits in the background with the door on the passenger side standing open. I assume the Model A belonged to my grandfather, that my father borrowed it, that he is the one who opened the door for this young woman in the sleeveless dress and flapper hat who is not as pretty as my mother.

My father is the boy in the starched white shirt with sleeves rolled to his elbow and pleated trousers that break just so over his shoes at the ankles. He is lanky, long-waisted, all muscle and bone and long legs with a felt hat that is tilted at a rakish angle.

He is not handsome. His features are too rugged and uneven for that definition, but he is attractive. His face is smooth, free of the wrinkles, saggy skin, and ruddy complexion that it later acquired from long hours in the hot sun. He wears an impish, devil-may-care expression that is as unfamiliar to me now as I would have been to him then.

He has not thought of me. He has not even met my mother, has not yet been introduced to the world of budgets and paychecks, midnight colic and baby bottles, prom dresses, slumber parties, and father-daughter banquets. He has not yet debated whether to buy savings bonds or to put money into a savings account to send me to college.

I feel deprived when I look at this picture. I feel as if I have come into the theater in the middle of a movie and missed something important.

I had this same feeling once before, when I was five years old and attended the funeral of a distant relative with my parents, and a woman with red lips, wearing a fur coat and alligator pumps with high heels threw her arms around my father's neck, left a lipstick print on his cheek, and addressed him as "Hugh Baby."

I had the same feeling then that I have each time I look at this photograph. I am jealous of the women who loved this younger version of my father.

# PAT WILLIAMS

## *Spirit Birth*

**D**eep creases etch the old man's leathery skin, weather worn and time spent. He crouches, hunched over a piece of marble, tapping, delicately chiseling another creation. Tourists pass, their indifferent glances scanning completed pieces. Unnoticed, he becomes simply another piece in the collection. He awaits sunset, eyes cast downward, oblivious to the crowd. Though years have passed he remembers her still, traces every detail again, preparing for his evening labor. He remembers the day she stopped at his stall and stood statuesque, small wisps of hair gently brushing her cheeks in the morning breeze. Her hair, fire red, cascaded over her shoulders flashing glints of gold under the Mexican sun. Handling a smooth marble dove, he knew she asked the price, but when his eyes met hers, he saw in them the shimmering emerald of the sea and offered her the piece. He held her eyes in his as long as she would allow. Then she smiled and walked to the next stall, holding his gift gingerly in one hand.

After dark, he enters the cave, lowering the torch to the earth floor. The flame illuminates his life's creation, sculpted from his most treasured block of marble. Tonight, standing back, he allows himself a reverent gaze upon this his yet unfinished masterpiece. She stands slightly taller than he is, her hair, framing a slender patrician face and spilling forward over bare alabaster shoulders. Her head tilts, eyes deep-set cast downward over rounded breasts as if she is leaning from her waist. One slender arm hangs delicately at her side, fingers clutching a hammer. The other arm bent, and in the hand, a chisel. Francisco's eyes travel slowly down the form past her knees to the still rough-hewn piece of marble. Soon, she will free herself completely.

191

SHARON E. YOUNG

# The Gift of Music

Johnny played his French horn at the elementary school, sat first chair through junior high and high school, marched as drum major in the county band, and visited the old folks home. I remember because no one in our small town cared much for the sound of music that coursed its way through the brass curls of the gold-toned horn. I remember because that sound of music sent me soaring over the disappointment of cerebral palsy that coursed its way through the sinews of my being. When Johnny played, any storm that raised its roar of thundering was stilled, as pure tone flew like a dream sequence to my tired mind. I could be whatever the music played, and I could master the art of being, no matter what the surge of lightning threat might bring. Johnny never complained when I asked him to play the aria again. He sang a solace through the twisted maze of brass, and sent the music up and to a heaven somewhere, where clouds are stages and big sky is arena and stars are the weary that have flown past gravity in search of peace. Johnny played and I listened, and even though we grew up in Julesburg, we grew up with kings and queens and courtiers that sang. No matter where or what or how much money sat in pockets, Johnny knew how rich we were, and he shared his wealth for free.

# Contributors' Notes

**V.T. ABERCROMBIE (Houston):** Her poems have appeared in literary magazines such as *Roanoke Review, White Rock Review, Bluegrass Literary Review, Rising Star, Slant, Madison Review, Pudding, Raintown Review, Pleiades, American Poets & Poetry, Borderlands, Illya's Honey, Visions International* and several anthologies. Pudding House published her chapbook, *Greatest Hits* in 2001. Co-Editor *Christmas in Texas,* Co-Author *Catering in Houston, Places to Take a Crowd in Houston,* author of *Houston Party File.*

**JUNE ADLER (Houston):** She is a visual artist and writer. Five of her short plays have been produced and she is currently working on a book of short stories.

**ANN K. ANDERSON (Conroe):** Ann is a published non-fiction writer and journalist now concentrating on fiction. A Yankee by birth, she lived abroad for twenty years and used those experiences in writing three novels set in Africa. She is now compiling a series of essays and short stories based on time spent in Tunisia. Her fiction has appeared in *Amelia Magazine* and several *Suddenly* anthologies and her poetry can be found on-line at *The Journals* www.the-journals.org.

**EVELYN CORRY APPELBEE (Henderson):** She is a native Texas poet whose work has appeared in national and international literary journals and anthologies, including *Behold Texas, Re:Arts and Letters,* (SFASU), *From Hide and Horn* (Eakin Press), *Concho River Review* and others. She and Violette Newton, Beaumont, co-authored *Letters from Two Women.* Evelyn's latest book is *Land where My Fathers Died,* poems from her diary as a U.S. Marine Corps Women's Reserve soldier.

**NICK ARGUELLO (Houston):** Nick teaches school in Houston.

**WILLIAM McCARGO BARNES (The Woodlands):** He is a retired geologist whose writing has appeared in the *2001 Anthology* published by the Panhandle Professional Writers Guild of Amarillo, in *Suddenly IV* and the "State Lines" section of the *Houston Chronicle.*

**CAROL BARRETT (Washington):** Carol Barrett is on the faculty of Union Institute & University in Cincinnati. Previously a resident of Corpus Christi and San Antonio, she won the 2002 Richard Snyder Memorial Publication Prize from Ashland Poetry Press; her winning manuscript *Calling In The Bones* will be released in 2003. *Drawing Lessons* (Poems) was published in 2002 by Finishing Line Press, and *The Unauthorized Book of Esther* (Poems) is coming out from Micah Publications.

**D. CREASON BARTLETT (Dallas):** He teaches in Dallas, is the editor of *Sojourn: A Journal of the Arts* and is co-founding editor of *Scriptorium Journal.*

**SUNDAY BENNETT (Rosenberg):** She is a freelance writer and artist who has been published in *Suddenly III,* the *Houston Chronicle* and *Controversy Magazine.* Besides writing and doing collage work she shares her life with seventeen pampered felines, two dogs and a husband who should be assigned sainthood.

**OVON ROSS BOOTH (Friendswood):** Ovon is a life member and councilor for the Poetry Society of Texas, a two time first prize winner at the Lucidity Conference in Eureka Springs and winner of many contests at local and state levels. She has been nominated for the Pushcart Award.

**KAY MERKEL BORUFF (Dallas):** Kay lived in Việt Nàm from 1968 to 1970 when her husband, who piloted for Air America, a division of the CIA, was killed. She has taught at The Hockaday School in Dallas since 1973, and her work has appeared in several journals and magazines.

**ANN REISFELD BOUTTÉ (Houston):** She was a juried poet in the 2001 Houston Poetry Fest. Her work has appeared in *Suddenly IV, My Table, Lilliput Review, Texas Poetry Calendar 2000, 2001, 2002,* and other publications. She is a former feature writer for a national wire service.

**ROBERTA PIPES BOWMAN: (Fort Worth):** Roberta is the author of eight books of poetry, one of which is the 1995 Lucidity Chapbook Award, and she is the 1998 Hilton Ross Greer Award winner from the Poetry Society of Texas. Recent publications include *descant* (TCU), *New Texas 2000, Galaxy of Verse, Poets' Forum, NFSP Encore 2001.*

196

**MICHAEL BRACKEN (Waco):** Michael is the editor of *Fedora: Private Eyes and Tough Guys* and the author of *All White Girls, Deadly Campaign, Psi Cops,* and more than 700 shorter works. His short stories have appeared in numerous magazines and anthologies, including *New Texas 2001* and *Suddenly IV.*

**BOB BRADLEY (Sugar Land):** Bob is the author of *How to Survive Your Bipolar Brain.* He is often the keynote speaker for CEU classes on anger management. His book, *17 Ways to Get from Rage to Reality,* will be available this fall. He recently had a piece in "State Lines" in the *Houston Chronicle.* He lives in Houston with his wife Lynn and their yellow Lab Gus.

**LYNN BRADLEY (Sugar Land):** Lynn, author of *Set Sail for Murder, Manic Depression: How to Live While Loving a Manic Depressive* and *TIPS for Beginning Fiction Writers,* lives in Houston with her husband Bob and their yellow Lab Gus.

**JUDY BRAND (Sugar Land):** She is a writer and visual artist whose work has appeared in *Texas Short Fiction, A World in Itself II, Suddenly III,* and other anthologies. "White Russian," a short story, was recently accepted for publication in *Sojourn.*

**MARTHA EVERHART BRANIFF (Houston):** Her short story, "Resurrection," is nominated for the 2002 Pushcart Prize. Her screenplay, "Sold," won The Actor's Choice Award. Her work has appeared in *Happy, Suddenly, Sojourn, Texas Poetry, Houston Chronicle, Village News, Texas Writer, New Texas, Women in Literary Arts Anthology* and others.

**ELIZABETH BRATTEN (Houston):** Elizabeth is a native of Tybee Island, Georgia. She received a B.A. in English from the University of Houston. Her work has appeared in the anthologies, *Christmas in Texas, The Leafraker,* and *Echoes for a New Room,* and most recently in "The Texas Writer." She is a charter member of The Friday Line, a continuing poetry workshop started in Houston in 1973.

**BILLIE LOU CANTWELL(Trinity):** She has published in journals such as TCU's *Descant, Borderlands, Texas Review, Sidewalks, Evangel, CQ, Rosebud, The Writer, Writer's Journal,* and *When I'm An Old Woman I Shall Wear Purple,* etc. She also conducts workshops at various Writer's Conferences.

**BIRMA CASTLE (Beaumont):** Birma is president of the Beaumont Poetry Society and is a councilor for the Poetry Society of Texas. She has been published in several PST Annual Awards anthologies, eight of Lucidity's ten Spring Conference anthologies, *In Celebration* and *A Galaxy of Verse.* She owned her own business and after retiring in 1990 finally had time for writing poetry. She is president of several other organizations and is a "Gift of Life" Breast Cancer Awareness Program volunteer and survivor speaker.

**PAMELYN CASTO (Granbury):** Pamelyn's articles have appeared in *Writer's Digest, The Art of Haiku 2000,* Web Del Sol's *Perihelion, Riding the Meridian, Fiction Fix, E2K, The New Literary Paradigm,* and the *Toastmaster.* Her shorter work has appeared in *Suddenly III, Potpourri, Modern Haiku, Ship of Fools, Mindprints* and other print and online publications. She runs online flash fiction and poetry workshops and teaches online courses in flash fiction.

**BETH LYNN CLEGG (Houston):** She is a fourth generation Texan whose fiction, nonfiction and poetry has appeared in numerous publications, including *Suddenly III* and *Suddenly IV.* Current work includes *Charity: True Stories of Giving and Receiving, A Cup of Comfort for Friends,* and *Women Forged in Fire.*

**SUZANNE C. COLE (Houston):** SuzAnne has been a Houstonian since 1972. She has published books, essays, poetry, plays, and fiction in many commercial and literary magazines, newspapers, and anthologies including *Newsweek, Houston Chronicle, USA Today, Troika, Personal Journaling,* and *Writing Your Life Story.* She also wrote *To Our Heart's Content: Meditations for Women Turning 50.*

**ELIZABETH CONLY (Cleburne):** She is now attending Pepperdine University, majoring in Theatre.

198

**GILDA MARY DADURA (Houston):** Originally from Connecticut, she has lived in Houston for twenty-seven years. She currently writes essays and stories and keeps an extensive journal of character portraits.

**BETTY DAVIS (Houston):** She is a freelance writer and editor, and has called Houston home since 1947. Her work has appeared in many journals and anthologies and is currently in *New Texas* as well as two Internet publications.

**PAULINE M. DELANEY (Houston):** Her work has appeared in several journals including *Suddenly II, III,* and *IV.*

**CANDACE DIMITRI (Wichita Falls):** She has lived and written in Texas for twenty years. She is a member and Councilor of the Poetry Society of Texas.

**WENDY DIMMETTE (Dallas):** She earned a M.A. from SMU with a creative thesis in poetry. She has published poetry in *Espejo, RE:artes Liberales, Poetry Society of Texas Yearbooks, Square Magazine, National Federation of State Poetry Societies, A Galaxy of Verse,* and other publications. Five children's plays have been performed at Cabbages and Kings Theatre for Children, and she has conducted poetry workshops at Eastfield College. She is the winner of the Pat Stodghill Book Publication Award 2002 published by Eakin Press.

**MARK A. EVANS (Houston):** Mark is a District Instructional Technology Teacher for the Klein Independent School District and is pursuing his Masters of Education in Curriculum and Technology from the University of Phoenix Online. He is a member of many educational, technology, and poetry organizations. One of his favorite hobbies is encouraging students to write and submit for contests and publications.

**YOLANDA FALCON (Houston):** She is a native Houstonian whose work has appeared in the *Houston Chronicle, Promise Magazine* and *Suddenly IV.* One of her essays was published in the *Women's Journal* in 2002. She also writes short plays and monologues.

**SUSAN LOVE FITTS (Montgomery):** She is a freelance writer with credits in the *Houston Chronicle*, other Texas newspapers and regional magazines. She is a member of the Woodlands Writers' Guild, SouthWest Writers, Writers' League of Texas, Poets Northwest, and the Poetry Society of Texas. Her first book of poetry *Licking the Bones Dry*, was published in 2001. She is currently the facilitator of "Poetry Nite Live," a monthly event at Barnes & Noble, The Woodlands.

**CAROLYN TOURNEY FLOREK (Houston):** She is a writer, visual artist and garden designer. She was born in Miami and grew up in Michigan and Iowa. After graduating with degrees in Geology and Fine Arts she moved to Houston. Her work has been published in *Suddenly III, IV,* and the *Houston Poetry Fest 2002* anthology.

**DEBORAH K. FRONTIERA (Houston):** Deborah is published in fiction, non-fiction and poetry. She teaches kindergarten in Houston ISD, but spends summers in her native Michigan's Upper Peninsula. She conducts workshops on writing for students, teachers and other writers. Visit her web site at www.authorsden.com/deborahkfrontiera.

**MARCIA GERHARDT (Houston):** She has published in prose poetry, short fiction and had a play produced as part of the Women's Playwriting Festival at Rice University in 1999. In 2000 she had a play reading at the Pasadena Little Theatre. In 2002 she received the Liam Cullen Award for Fiction writing, and her mystery book *Blood Diamond* was a finalist in the Writers' League of Texas manuscript contest for 2002.

**J. LEE GOODMAN (Wichita Falls):** She works for the Wichita Falls I.S.D. in the Science Resource Center and volunteers at her local nature center. She has been writing poetry since 1977 and is the current publicity chair for the Wichita Falls Chapter of the Poetry Society of Texas. A prose poem was published in *Suddenly IV.*

**JOHN GORMAN (Galveston):** John teaches literature and creative writing at UH-Clear Lake. His poetry, gathered in three chapbooks, has appeared in many places in the U.S. and Canada and he has contributed to all five *Suddenly* anthologies.

**NANCY GUSTAFSON (Huntsville):** Nancy has published poetry and short fiction in several anthologies and journals, including *Suddenly IV, Lucidity Poetry Journal, Inner Visions, A book of the Year* (Poetry Society of Texas) and *The Herbalist Journal.*

**JOYCE POUNDS HARDY (Houston):** Joyce is a native Houstonian and graduate of Rice University. *The Reluctant Hunter*, her first book of poetry was published with a winning grant from the Texas Commission on the Arts. Her non-fiction book, *Surviving Aunt Ruth* was published and released October 2002.

**JOHN HAYMAKER (Houston):** He is a web site developer and computer programmer residing in Houston. Other publications include op-ed articles, poetry and translations of Chinese short stories.

**LINNEA HEANEY (College Station):** She is a writer and teacher living in College Station. Someday she plans to sew a quilt. "Autumn Pieced Work" is her first published poem.

**JAMES HOGGARD (Wichita Falls):** He is the Perkins Prothro Distinguished Professor of English at Midwestern State University in Wichita Falls, and was named the Texas State Poet Laureate for 2000. A former NEA Fellow and past president of The Texas Institute of Letters, he has authored numerous literary works throughout his career, including essays, short stories, plays and hundreds of poems. Of his sixteen books published, his poetry book *Medea in Taos* (Pecan Grove Press) was nominated for the Violet Crown Award. *Rain in a Sunlit Sky* (Page One Publications) came out in 2000, and *Patterns of Illusion: Stories & a Novella* (Wings Press) was published in 2002.

**J. PAUL HOLCOMB (Double Oak):** "The Poet from Double Oak" is the immediate past President of the Poetry Society of Texas. He has authored one chapbook of poems, co-authored a children's book, and has over one hundred poems in various literary journals and anthologies. He is a retired software engineer.

**BARBARA J. HOLT (Friendswood):** She is a semi-retired teacher who has written miles of curriculum, various non-fiction articles and fiction. Her publications include *Galaxy, The Tower, The Social Studies Texan,* and *The Friendswood Journal.*

**PEPPER HUME Spring):** Her training as a writer consisted of reading— science fiction, historical, mystery, sword and sorcery, almost anything written in English. She is a member of the Woodlands Writers Guild and Writers in the Hat.

**JAMES HUSUM (The Woodlands):** James runs RIAH Software by day, creating Internet applications. By night he pounds the keyboard in an effort to release the pressure of stories inside him. He has been published in *Suddenly* previously.

**GUIDA JACKSON (The Woodlands):** Guida Jackson's publishers include Simon & Shuster and Oxford University Press. In 2000 she established Panther Creek Press to publish other writers. She has a B.A. in Journalism, M.A. in Third World Literature, Ph.D. in Comparative Literature.

**RONALD W. JAEGER (Austin):** Ron recently launched into full-time creative writing. His first published poem, "Wildflowers," appeared in *Suddenly III.* His first published short story, "Shimmering at Noon," appeared in *Futures Magazine.* His most recent story "P is for Ping," appeared in 2002 in *Palo Alto Review.*

**ANGÉLIQUE JAMAIL (Houston):** She is a native Houstonian and lives and writes in Texas most of the year. She earned a Creative Writing/ English degree from the University of Houston. Her first collection of poems, entitled *Gypsies,* came out in late 1998. Her second one, *Barefoot on Marble: Twenty Poems, 1995—2001* will be out in 2003.

**GRETCHEN LONG JAMESON (Houston):** She received a B.A. in English Literature in 1982 from the University of Colorado.She was born and has lived most of her life in Houston. Her joys are her husband, daughter, writing and helping others. She has published in *Suddenly IV* and *The Pedestal Magazine.*

**RAMONA JOHN (Crowley):** Ramona is a former Houston judge who is happily retired, and enjoying her new career as a writer. Her first book was *Children and the Law in Texas* (University of Texas Press 1999), and she has been published in various magazines and newspapers.

**CHARLOTTE JONES (Houston):** She is a writer and photographer. Her work has appeared or is forthcoming in several journals including *The Bellevue Literary Review, The Pedestal Magazine,* and *¡Tex!* where her story "Crossroads" tied for first place in a fiction contest. Her photography accompanied a recent Houston Symphony performance and has appeared in several children's magazines.

**CELE S. KEEPER (Houston):** Cele is a retired social worker who has been a laboratory technician, bookstore owner, university professor of human sexuality, and is still a political activist, fanatical theatre-goer, wife and mother.

**JULIE C. KEMPER (Houston):** She earned a B.A. in English and minored in Spanish. She is a sculptor, painter, writer of poetry, essays, and short stories. Recently a poem was published in *Texas Poetry Calendar 2000,* and she was in a PBS film, "Life Stories" in 2001.

**MARILYN GILBERT KOMECHAK (Fort Worth):** For twenty years Marilyn was a therapist in private practice. She has written several books including a children's book to be published this spring. Her books were presented at the Chicago Book Expo and the Austin Book Fair in 2001. She is a member of the Fort Worth Poetry Society and has had poems and short stories published in the U.S., Europe and Canada.

**WILLIAM LAUFER (The Woodlands):** He is a visual artist whose most recent publication credit is as cover artist and illustrator for *Watching the Worlds Go By,* a late collection of poetry by Omar S. Pound (Panther Creek Press, 2001). His poetry and fiction have appeared in previous *Suddenly* collections, and he is presently battling cancer.

**VIRGINIA LONG (Houston):** She has published four chapbooks , has appeared in numerous literary journals and anthologies and has won many awards in the Poetry Society of Texas annual contests.

**MARY ELAINE LORA (Houston):** A technical writer by day, Mary Elaine writes plays and fiction at night. She has had several one-act plays produced. Her first published short story, "Necessary Casualties," appeared in *Futures* in 2002 and won the magazine's Karen Besecker Award.

**PEGGY ZULEIKA LYNCH (Austin):** Peggy Lynch is a native Texan, Poet Laureate, Poet-in-Residence at the Paris American Academy and founder of Poetry in the Arts, Austin's longest running poetry venue. She has published in many publications and has authored nine books of poetry, co-authored six additional poetry books, and co-edited fifteen anthologies.

**ANNE McCRADY (Henderson):** She is an East Texas poet and story teller whose prize-winning work appears in both journals and anthologies. Her life and writing focus on the need for open-hearted living.

**BRIGID K. McVAUGH (Houston):** She is a writer and dietitian in Clear Lake where she has lived for eleven years. Her work has appeared in *the Houston Chronicle, The Hearty Appetite,* "This Week" and *The Arabian Advocate.*

**LIANNE ELIZABETH MERCER (Fredericksburg):** Lianne edits *The Texas Poetry Calendar* and is a Certified Poetry Therapist who leads workshops about how writing heals. Her short story, "For Sale," (which first appeared in *Suddenly III)* was nominated in 2001 by *Margins,* an online magazine, for a Pushcart Prize.

**BETH MILES (Huntsville):** Beth is a native Texan with a smalltown/ rural background, though she lived in Houston for many of her adult years. She is a member of Billie Lou Cantwell's writing group "The Raven's Quill" in Walker County.

**HALLIE MOORE (The Woodlands):** Her work has appeared in such journals as *Texas Review, Blue Mesa Review, Spillway, The Texas Magazine, Borderlands, Calyx* and others. She received a B.A. and M.A. from Stanford University and a MFA from Antioch University Los Angeles.

**RITA NESBITT (Trinity):** She is a lay minister and retired secretary, and has written a weekly humorous newspaper column on word roots/ meanings for eight years . The newspaper has published a Christmas story and several other items. She writes the newsletter for her church and belongs to a writer's critique group. She is working on several novels and a nonfiction guide for new Christians.

**REECE NEWTON (Cleona, PA):** He grew up in Beaumont, graduated from Lamar, taught college English and studied in Arizona and Illinois. He now writes and restores antique radios in his spare time. He lived and taught in Guatemala and Spain and has been published in *Suddenly III* and *Suddenly IV.*

**VIOLETTE NEWTON (Beaumont):** Violette Newton is one of twenty-five career women profiled in P.J. Pierce's *"Let me tell you what I've learned," TEXAS WISEWOMEN SPEAK* (Texas U. Press). She is a member of the Southeast Texas Womens' Hall of Fame, and is a much published and much honored Poet Laureate of Texas.

**REBECCA NOLEN (Sugar Land):** She is a member of the Fort Bend Writer's Guild and the Society of Children's Writers and Illustrators. She has had several articles published in magazines and has written three children's books and a novel.

**CLAIRE OTTENSTEIN-ROSS (Pinehurst):** Claire is an award winning poet and author of eleven books. She has published in *Touchstone, Who's Who in Texas Letters* and in magazines and anthologies in secular and inspiration circles. She is the retired President/Editor of Counterpoint Publishing Co., co-founder of Poets Northwest, Houston Northwest Inspirational Writers Alive! and Christian Writers Northwest. The 1998 Poetry Society of Texas Book of the Year was dedicated to her for promoting poetry in Texas.

**LISA L. POWELL (Houston):** She is a graduate of the University of Texas at Austin and the School of the Art Institute of Chicago. Currently, she is a grant writer at a large, non-profit art organization. She is a new fiction/poetry writer and filmmaker, and these are her first published works.

**CARLYN LUKE REDING (Austin):** She is a sixth generation Texan with Native American roots. She was born in Freeport, lived in Lake Jackson and taught in the Brazosport School District before moving to Austin. She is a member of the Writers' League of Texas and the Austin International Poetry Festival and is published in *3 Savanna Blue* and *Red Boots and Attitude.*

**RUTH E. REUTHER (Wichita Falls):** She is a native Texan and was named Poet Laureate of Texas in 1987. She was also nominated for the best children's book by the Texas Institute of Letters and has published eight books and over four hundred articles.

**CAROL J. RHODES (Houston):** Carol's works of poetry, short stories, essays and non-fiction have appeared in numerous magazines, newspapers, journals, anthologies and business publications. Recent acceptances include *New Texas 2001, Soujourn, Texas* Magazine, and *The Christian Science Monitor.* Her poetry and essays have appeared in *Suddenly I, II, III,* and *IV.*

**ALVARO RODRIGUEZ (Galveston):** Alvaro is a native Texan. His recent publications include *The Mesquite Review, Marrow, flashquake* and *In Posse Review.* His short story, "Son of the Hawk," is a 2003 Pushcart Prize nominee.

**JANE BUTKIN ROTH (Houston):** Roth's poetry, essays and fiction have appeared in over seventy publications, including the *Houston Chronicle, Oklahoma Today, Suddenly, Nerve Cowboy*, and the anthologies *Haiku-Sine, Essential Love, Mothers and Daughters* and *Baby Blessings.* Her book *We Used to Be Wives: Divorce Unveiled Through Poetry* by Fithian Press, June 2002, is an anthology of poems by over seventy women who have experienced divorce.

**DONALD WALTER SAMP (Spring):** He studied creative writing for several years at Rice University. His selection titled "Caged Spirit" received an Honorable Mention at the 2000 Golden Triangle Writer's Guild Conference in Beaumont.

**NAOMI STROUD SIMMONS (Fort Worth):** She is active in local poetry groups, conducts workshops for eighth grade and high school creative writing classes, is Director for the Poetry Society of Texas and has had poems published in *Galaxy, Lucidity, Grassland, New Texas, NFSPS* and the Poetry Society of Texas Year Books.

**THOMAS SPIRITI (Missouri City):** He is originally from Mississippi but has lived in the Houston area since 1992. He earned a B.A. in English from Spring Hill College in Mobile, AL and a M.A. in Liberal Arts from St. Thomas University, Houston. He writes full-time and is working on a novel based on "Sarah's Detour."

**CATHY STERN (Houston):** She received a M.A. in English and Creative Writing from the University of Houston, and the Pen Southwest Award for Poetry in 1985. Her work has been published in *The Paris Review, The New Republic,* and *Shenandoah*, and poems and an interview appeared in the anthology *A Wider Giving: Women Writing After A Long Silence*, (Chicory Blue Press, 1988). She has taught English and Creative Writing at UH-Downtown and poetry workshops for adults at the community level.

**SANDI STROMBERG (Houston):** Sandi is an award winning writer and poet with over 350 stories, essays and articles published in the U.S. and Europe (where she lived for twenty years). She teaches writing classes regularly at the Jung Center in Houston and annually at the International Women's Writing Guild Summer Conference in New York. Her poetry translations have appeared in *i.e. magazine* and *Linguisticum* (Luxembourg).

**ELLYN TORNES (The Woodlands):** Ellyn has lived in the Houston area for over twenty years where she writes fiction and poetry.

**STEPHEN VILLARI (Fort Worth):** He is currently attending Fort Worth Country Day. He has been writing for two years and "The Real World" is is his first entry to an anthology. He enjoys kayaking and fast cars, and plans to use his creative skills to make movies, etc.

**BEV VINCENT (The Woodlands):** He is an active member in the Horror Writers Association, writes "News from the Dead Zone" for *Cemetery Dance* magazine and has published over one hundred book reviews in the *Conroe Courier.* His stories have appeared in *Octoberland, Peep Show, Suddenly IV, The Harrow, Royal Aspirations III* and *The Archives of Arrissia.* View his current credits at http://www.BevVincent.com.

**SUE PETERS VOLK (Houston):** She grew up in Denver and attended the University of Colorado, later graduating in piano performance from Wichita State University. Her work has appeared in *Suddenly III* and *Suddenly IV.*

**LORETTA DIANE WALKER (Odessa):** Her work has appeared in magazines, journals and anthologies such as *Verses Magazine, The Odessa America, The Duster, Udder Tales, Journey into Writing, Boy's Quest Magazine,* the anthologies *Seasons to Come, Between the Raindrops, Best Poems of 1996, Best in Poetry, Promises to Keep, A Time to Be Free, Poetry Contest 1998, Cross Roads* and many other publications. She is an elementary music teacher at Reagan Elementary Magnet School in Odessa.

**GERALD R. WHEELER (Katy):** His photography, fiction and poetry have appeared in *Whole Terrain, Yemassee, Oregon Review, Sunstone, Potomac Review, Vincent Brothers Review, Descant, Louisiana Literature, Pivot* and elsewhere. He is the author of *Tracers.* His poetry collection *Tracks* was published by Timberline Press in 2002. He was nominated for the Puscart in short fiction in 2002.

**CYNTHIA K. WIER (Houston):** A Central Texas native, she has been writing poetry, short fiction and essays for ten years. In 2001 her poems appeared in the *Texas Poetry Calendar* and *My Kitchen Table,* and short short fiction in *Suddenly IV.* A holiday trip inspired her recent work: the art and architecture of Rome, Sorrento and Pompeii and the castles near Munich.

**BETTY WIESEPAPE (Richardson):** She is Assistant Director of Creative Writing at the University of Texas at Dallas in Richardson where she teaches literature and creative writing. Betty holds a Ph.D. in literature, writes short stories, creative nonfiction, academic articles and book reviews. Her work has appeared in *Southwestern Historical Quarterly, Dallas Morning News, Blue Mesa Review, New Texas, Texas Short Fiction I, Just a Moment Quarterly, Riversedge, Concho Review* and *Suddenly.* An essay on her work along with a short story has been selected for inclusion in a book on Texas women writers of short stories soon to be released from Texas A&M Press.

**PAT WILLIAMS (Houston):** She was formerly a writing and English teacher and currently serves as a parent educator for the Aldine Independent School District, assisting in the facilitation of a parenting program at Head Start and Pre-Kindergarten centers. She is a freelance writer with credits including *The Houston Chronicle, Church Educator, Patchwork Poetry, Suddenly, Suddenly II* and *Unsent Letters* an anthology selected for the July 2002 Writer's Digest Book Club.

**SHARON E. YOUNG (Houston):** She is a published poet, a member of the Poetry Society of Texas and currently president of Poets Northwest in Houston. She is also director of a new publishing company, is the mother of three grown children, and resides in Houston with her husband Robert.

# Colophon

*Suddenly V*, consisting of 212 pages, was edited and typeset on a Power Macintosh G3 using Times New Roman and Zap Chancery fonts. The cover was designed by Jesse Johnson and the book was printed and perfect bound by Morgan Printing, Austin, Texas.

*Suddenly is an independently published anthology with the purpose of showcasing Texas authors. No monetary rewards are received from individuals or organizations other than through sale of yearly publications.*

Order copies of

*Suddenly 98 - ISBN 0-9627844-2-7*
*Suddenly II - ISBN 0-9627844-3-5*
*Suddenly III - ISBN 0-9627844-4-3*
*Suddenly IV - ISBN 0-9627844-7-8*
*Suddenly V - ISBN 0-9627844-9-4*

from

Stone River Press
2003 Corral Drive, Houston, TX 77090
ph: 281-440-6701  fax: 281-440-7975
www.stoneriverpress.com

*Suddenly V* is $10.00 plus .0725 Texas tax
and $2.00 shipping—add 50 cents shipping for each
additional book. Back issues are $6.00 each plus tax and
shipping as above.

~~~ www.stoneriverpress.com ~~~